D1706482

99 Ways

to take control of your

Anxiety &

Stress

Wendy Becker, LCSW

© 2015 Wendy Becker, LCSW
First Printing 2015

ISBN 13: 978-0-692-32391-5
Library of Congress Control Number: 2015902345
Kamgan Publishing
Fort Collins, Colorado

www.WendyBeckerLCSW.com

Printed in the United States of America

Cover Design: 99Designs.com
Adi Bustaman / www.AdiBustamanDesign.com
Cover Photos: Hanna Slavinska / ©123RF.com

Publisher's Note

Neither the publisher nor the author is engaged in rendering medical or mental health advice to the reader. Nothing in this book is intended as a substitute for professional medical or mental health treatment. You should always seek the assistance of a licensed professional for your personal health needs. Neither the author nor the publisher shall be liable or responsible in any way for any loss or damage allegedly arising from any information or advice in this book.

Darkness cannot live in the light

For Logan and Kameran,
The two brightest lights in my world

Contents

Acknowledgements xi

Introduction 1

Managing Your Thoughts, Feelings & Emotions 7

   #1 Understand What You Are Dealing With 9

   #2 Don't Be a Victim of Victim Thinking 10

   #3 Change the Channel 11

   #4 Use Your "What If" Powers for Good 13

   #5 Visualize Your Stress and Anxiety 14

   #6 Don't Take Things Personally 16

   #7 Check the Evidence 17

   #8 Be a Duck 18

   #9 Learn to Manage Your Anger 19

   #10 Don't Compare 21

   #11 Don't Be Afraid to Fail 22

   #12 Be Patient 23

   #13 Accept Change 24

   #14 Have Good Boundaries 25

   #15 Let Go of the Past 26

   #16 Focus on the Positive 27

   #17 Not Everyone Has to Like You 28

   #18 Forgive 29

   #19 Focus on What You Can Control 30

#20 See the Best in Others 31

#21 Talk Nicely to Yourself 32

#22 Let Go of Perfectionist Thinking 33

#23 Know the Difference between Helping & Being a Doormat . 34

#24 Don't Avoid 35

#25 Let Go of Control 36

#26 Pick Your Battles 37

#27 Use Fair Fighting Skills 38

#28 Look for Exit Ramps 39

#29 Find Your But 40

#30 Take Charge of Your Own Happiness 41

#31 Accept Yourself 42

#32 Know Your Triggers 43

#33 Eustress vs. Distress 44

#34 Think Before You Speak 45

#35 Know Where You Are on the Escalation Scale 46

#36 Be Aware (and Beware) of Secondary Stress 48

#37 Deal with Your Past 49

#38 Acknowledge Your Feelings 50

#39 Play the Odds with Worry 51

#40 Have Reasonable Goals 52

#41 Focus on the Present 53

#42 Don't Sabotage Yourself 54

#43 Boost Your Self-Esteem 55

#44 Don't Overreact 56

Things You Can Do to Conquer Anxiety & Stress 59

#45 Practice Relaxation Breathing 61

#46 Manage or Eliminate Unhealthy Relationships 63

#47 Be Assertive, Not Aggressive 65

#48 Walk Away 66

#49 Say I'm Sorry 67

#50 Indulge in Guilty Pleasures 69

#51 Find a Hobby... 70

#52 Reach Out and Accept Help................................... 71

#53 Say No... 71

#54 Limit Negative Input 72

#55 Use Positive Affirmations 73

#56 Do Something Nice for Yourself 74

#57 Volunteer Somewhere 75

#58 Spend Time with Friends 76

#59 Take a Mental Health Day 76

#60 Do Yoga... 77

#61 Visualize a Calming Place..................................... 78

#62 Get a Massage 79

#63 Do Something Nice for Someone 80

#64 Spend Some Time in Nature................................... 81

#65 Progressive Muscle Relaxation................................ 82

#66 Take a Time-Out 82

#67 Live for Yourself... 83

#68 Take a 5-Minute Vacation 84

#69 Count Your Blessings 85

#70 Use a Mantra for Deep Breathing 86

#71 Journal 87

#72 Escape into a Good Movie or TV Show.................... 88

#73 Plant and Care for a Garden 88

#74 Take a Warm Bath 89

#75 Throw Some Tissues 89

#76 Cook Something 90

#77 Color in a Coloring Book 91

#78 Read a Good Book 91

#79 Listen to Music 92

#80 Dance 93

#81 Pet Your Dog (or Cat)..................................... 93

#82 Laugh 94

#83 Delegate.. 95

Lifestyle Changes to Manage Anxiety & Stress 97

#84 Eat a Healthy Diet... 99

#85 Exercise.. 100

#86 Get Enough Sleep 101

#87 Get Organized.. 102

#88 Work at a Job You Like 104

#89 Stop Procrastinating 105

#90 Have Good Time Management 106

#91 Adopt a Spiritual Practice 107

#92 Have an End-of-the- Workday Ritual...................... 108

#93 Learn Healthy Coping Skills 109

#94 Have a Good Support System and Use It.................. 110

#95 Evaluate Where You Spend Your Time 112

#96 Balance Your Wheel of Life 113

#97 Take It Easy on the Caffeine 114

#98 Take a Break during the Workday 115

#99 Get Professional Help 116

References 119

About the Author 123

Acknowledgements

I am so thankful to the Divine who has put so many wonderful blessings and people in my life. I am especially grateful for those who helped me bring this project to life.

Laura Garrett, I am thankful that you are my friend. You have helped to push me and motivate me, and I would not have written this book without you, nor would my life (and my Friday nights) be as fun.

Jennifer Top, my editor and friend. Thank you for all of your help and for just being you. You never cease to make me smile and laugh.

My beautiful parents, Jack and Rita. Thank you for always believing in me and helping me to believe in myself and for always being there.

And to my husband, Vince. Your love and support mean everything to me.

Thank you also to the many people I have had the honor of working with throughout the years. You inspire me with your strength and commitment to beating anxiety and stress. I am honored to be part of your journey.

Adopting the right attitude can convert a
negative stress into a positive one.
—Hans Selye

Introduction

Everyone experiences some anxiety and stress. We live in a fast-paced, sometimes crazy-busy society that does not value enough the importance of relaxation and down time. Although we all have some stress and worry, when they begin to affect your ability to function in your daily life, it is a warning sign that you need to take action now to manage your life. Some of the ways your daily life can be affected include having trouble focusing or concentrating at work or school, experiencing difficulty getting to sleep and staying asleep (or sleeping too much), finding it hard to eat (or eating too much), or having any of the above interfere with your relationships, your mood, your job, or your health.

When stress and worry become chronic, it can cause a multitude of physical and mental health issues. If you don't learn to manage your stress and worry properly, some of those issues can become very serious. In fact, stress causes and makes worse nearly every physical and mental disorder on the planet. That is scary! Unmanaged stress can lead to cardiovascular disease, gastrointestinal problems, an impaired immune system, accelerated aging, depression and anxiety disorders, and other serious health issues. Stress has also been linked to impaired memory and Alzheimer's.

You might think that stress is more of a mental thing, like a state of mind or a feeling. Stress is actually both a mental and a physical issue. All sorts of interesting things happen in your body when you are stressed. When your body and mind perceive something as a threat, your body prepares to deal with whatever the threat is by sending messages throughout your body to be on alert and be ready to fight or flee (fight or flight response). This happens through your central nervous system.

Your body's central nervous system is divided into two parts: the sympathetic and the parasympathetic. When you are calm and relaxed, your parasympathetic nervous system is in control. But, when you are stressed and anxious, your sympathetic nervous system is in control. The sympathetic nervous system's job is to help you prepare to face danger and deal with stress. It does this by releasing stress hormones such as cortisol, epinephrine, and adrenaline that can help you deal with the danger. Your eyesight changes in ways that help you see better, blood flows to certain parts of your body like your brain, hands and feet are redirected, your gastrointestinal system changes, your heart rate and blood pressure go up, and breathing becomes shallow and quick. These physiological processes can make you feel panicked, or like you are having a heart attack, especially when there is no obvious sign of a threat.

If your stress is chronic, that constant demand on your body's systems can exhaust your body's reserves. It is this repeated demand on your body and mind that leads to disease and impairs your ability to heal from illness. It is very important that you learn how to manage your worry and stress to give your body's systems a chance to rest and recoup.

This book was written to give you many different ways to manage your anxiety and stress, all of which are based in cognitive behavioral therapy (CBT) strategies. It is organized into three sections. The first section helps you learn to change how you think (cognitions) to manage your anxiety and stress. The second part gives you tools to help you with behaviors that can decrease anxiety and stress, and the third part is about lifestyle changes you can make that will also improve your ability to fight stress and anxiety.

My hope is that you will read this book and find a variety of ideas you can incorporate into your life to get your anxiety and stress under control. Not every tool is going to work for every person, but I guarantee there is something in here for everyone. I also hope this will be a resource for you in times when stress and anxiety feel out of control—a lifeline that you can reach for to find something that will work in the moments when you feel overwhelmed and don't know what to do.

If you are not sure how to incorporate these strategies into your life, talk with a professional about how you can make them work for you. This book is not meant to replace professional help. It is meant to be a tool you can use in your fight against anxiety and stress—a fight you can win.

You are never powerless over stress and anxiety, though it can sometimes feel that way. You deserve to be happy

and live life according to your own terms, and this book
can help you do that.

Many Blessings to You.

—Wendy

Whether you think you can, or you think you can't—you're right.

—Henry Ford

Managing Your Thoughts, Feelings & Emotions

#1
Understand What You Are Dealing With

With anxiety and stress, knowledge truly is power. When you understand what is going on in your body, you can think of your symptoms in a different way. Understanding the physiological reactions that occur when you are stressed or having a panic attack can help you make sense of what is occurring. You will know that it is not something you are doing wrong and it is not a weakness or character flaw of some sort that makes you feel this way. This knowledge can also help you figure out what you need to do to manage your symptoms.

First, what is stress? Stress is the non-specific response to a demand on the body's systems. It is non-specific because different things can cause stress to different people. And, there is no specific response by the body's systems because we all react to stress differently.

Anxiety is defined in a lot of different ways, but anxiety is basically a future-oriented state of mind in which a person prepares for the possibility of bad things happening. The fear associated with anxiety is a perception of danger, which can be real or imagined. Anxiety is about what **might** happen and our fear of it happening.

People experience stress and anxiety in different ways. To begin to control them, you have to pay attention to what you feel in your body as well as the thoughts you have when you feel stressed and anxious. This knowledge can help you recognize symptoms before you feel overwhelmed so you can start taking evasive action right away and prevent those symptoms from taking over. This knowledge can also help you identify which tools work best for you and when to use them. Just like people experience stress and anxiety differently, some tools might work better for you than others.

Keeping a log of your thoughts, feelings, physical symptoms, and what was going on before you began to feel your symptoms can help you identify patterns and triggers. Keeping track of what tools you use can also help you know what works best for you. Remember that stress and anxiety do not necessarily happen because of something you are doing wrong, but with your new knowledge, you might find that you can do things differently that will help you stop and better cope with your anxiety and stress.

#2
Don't Be a Victim
of Victim Thinking

Stress and anxiety can feel so overwhelming at times that you might feel you have no control over them and that nothing you can do will ever make things better. When we feel we have no control over something that is happening to us and even within us, we can feel like a victim. Being a victim makes us feel powerless, but this could not be further from the truth. You have so much more power and control over your stress and anxiety than you can imagine.

Taking charge of your body and your mind by using the techniques in this book, working with a therapist, taking medication if necessary, making lifestyle changes, or any combination of these can help you effectively manage your thoughts and emotions and take hold of your power.

Your number one belief must be that you—not your anxiety and stress—are in charge of you, and you will make your life what you want it to be. Stress and anxiety will try to confuse and control you, but never forget that you are stronger. You can take charge of your life and push through this, coming out on the other side to a happier and healthier life.

#3
Change the Channel

How many times have you caught yourself thinking the same thoughts over and over, ruminating on something that stresses you out? Worrying about a situation, a relationship, your health, or whatever else is bothering you? This is very common with both stress and anxiety.

I think of it as a television running constantly inside of your head, and whatever we are thinking about is what channel it is on. Sometimes you might get on the Anxiety channel and ruminate on what ifs, such as what if my partner is cheating on me or what if something bad happens. Or if you're feeling depressed, you can get on the Sadness channel and focus only on those things that make you sad. If you've experienced a trauma, you might find yourself getting stuck on the channel that keeps you repeatedly going over and over what happened to you. It can be the same if you're angry. You can get stuck on the Anger channel and continuously think thoughts that feed your anger.

We all have channels in our heads that we can get stuck on from time to time, but you don't have to stay there. If I were to tell you to simply stop thinking about what is bothering you, you might say, "yeah, right!" or "I've tried! It's not that easy!" I would agree with you. However, I've found that if you think of it as your own unhealthy channel you're getting stuck on, it makes it easier to visualize how to change your thoughts if I told you to change your channel to a healthier one.

To change your channel, you have to create a channel that is good for you to think about—a channel that you enjoy and one that is healthier for you to focus on. For example, if you enjoy gardening, you could create a Gardening channel where you can think about how you are going to plant a flower or vegetable garden. You can plan out where you will plant, what types of plants and seeds you will need, and the order in which you will plant everything. You can think about where the sun will shine on your beds to maximize efficiency when you plan, the watering schedule and system you will use, and so on.

When you find yourself on the Anxiety channel, visualize switching to the Gardening channel. Visualize everything about what you want to do in your garden and imagine just how it will look when everything starts growing. This is a much healthier channel to be on and can be both relaxing and something you have control over. The more you practice this skill, the easier you will find it to change the channel when you feel anxious.

Just recently I was talking to a friend who was going through a painful breakup with a longtime boyfriend. She found herself often on her Sad channel, ruminating on her pain and grief from the breakup. As a small business owner, she was able to create a Work channel in which she focused on what she needed to do at work and how she could do it. This was real, tangible, and something she could accomplish that meant a lot to her. It didn't mean she didn't go through the grief process, but she stopped allowing herself to get stuck in it, which helped her to move on.

It is impossible not to think, but you can control what you think about. Take a moment or two to think about what type of channel would be good for you. Really imagine what you would see, hear, smell, touch, and perhaps even taste. You can create more than one channel you can go to when you find yourself on your unhealthy channel. There are many different types of Negative Thoughts channels, but there are infinite amounts of Positive Thoughts channels. You just have to find yours and go to it (or them) as often as possible.

#4
Use Your "What If" Powers for Good

I use this one all the time with my clients, my family, my friends, and myself. I took this technique from my mother because she often used it on me while I was growing up and even as an adult when I talk to her about things. Every single time I say something to her such as "What if I can't?" or "What if it doesn't work?" she asks me, "What if you can?" and "What if it does work?"

What if thinking can really stress us out and increase anxiety because when we think of all the future possibilities, we ask ourselves what if questions a lot. Most people will think of all the worst-case scenarios about the things that could happen and allow their imaginations to come up with scary possibilities and outcomes. This is not healthy thinking, and what we worry about most usually does not happen.

To combat what if thinking, use your what if powers for good. Every time you catch yourself thinking a negative what if thought, think a positive what if thought. For example, if you have to give a speech at work or school you might think, "What if I get up there and sound like an idiot?" Then immediately challenge that negative thought by saying to yourself, "What if I get up there and do a great job?" "What if this helps me get that promotion I'm up for?" If you have done a good job preparing for your speech, you will feel more confident. Talking positively to yourself will further help to build your confidence, thereby decreasing anxiety and stress. Your positive self-talk helps to increase the likelihood that you will do well, too.

#5
Visualize Your Stress and Anxiety

Stress and anxiety are thought of as feelings or emotions inside of you, but if you pictured them outside of your body and mind, what would you see? Try and give your stress or anxiety a size, a shape, a color, and even a face. Does it have arms or legs? Visualize it in your mind or draw it on paper.

Some of the things I have heard from clients who have tried this technique are that the color is black or gray, it looks like a monster or a little fuzzy blob, and that it takes countless other types of shapes. Not surprising is that neither stress nor anxiety is ever pleasant-looking or appears friendly in any way.

Once you have positioned your stress or anxiety outside of you rather than as something that is a part of you, you can take charge of it in a new way. Tell it to sit down and be quiet. Tell it that you are in charge and are no longer going to let it run your life. Maybe you can even make it look a little less scary by making it rainbow colored or changing its appearance in any way that makes sense to you. Have fun with it as you take control.

Visualize your stress or anxiety and then imagine there is a box beside it. The box can be big, little, fancy, simple, colorful, or anything else you feel would securely contain your stress/anxiety. Some might change this box to a suitcase, a trunk with straps, or any other container that makes sense to you. Then add a big lock to it, for which only you have the key.

Once you can visualize your box or container, look again at your stress or anxiety and see it shrinking small enough to fit in the box. Take as long as you need. It might resist shrinking, but you are the one in charge and you can make it shrink. I had one person tell me that their stress did not want to shrink and was making a lot of noise so they imagined putting tape over its mouth and then it was easier to make it shrink. Like I said, be as creative as you need to be to make it fit in the box.

Once you have shrunk it down and put it in the box, you can choose what to do with the box. You can tape it up, put it in a closet, bury it in the backyard, or do whatever you choose. You can do whatever you want because this is your visualization and you are the one in charge. It doesn't always feel like you are the one in charge when stress and anxiety feel overwhelming, but you can take charge and this is a great technique to help you remember that.

#6
Don't Take Things Personally

Some people who are highly stressed and anxious tend to pay a lot of attention to what others think, say, and do, and take those things personally. It can help if you remember that not everything is about you, though.

We've all had the experience where a friend doesn't respond in a way we think he or she should and we take it personally. For those who are highly anxious or stressed, you might be on high alert and misinterpret cues from others, making their reactions about you because you are so worried about what other people think. This is particularly true for people with social anxiety.

But unless you have a crystal ball or can read minds, you don't know what causes people to behave the way they do, so why would you automatically assume it is about you? This type of thinking can become an unhealthy habit, which will only increase your stress and anxiety. So let things go. We have enough to contend with focusing on our own thoughts and emotions; we don't need to take responsibility for others' feelings and actions.

#7
Check the Evidence

This technique can help you challenge anxious, stressful thoughts and beliefs. How many times have you had worry and stressful thoughts about something that may happen in the future or fears about what other people think of you? These types of thoughts are very common for those with stress and anxiety.

Someone who has their annual work evaluation coming up may start getting nervous about it weeks in advance. Some worry in this situation is normal, but what can be unhealthy is if that normal worry morphs into a downward spiral: thoughts that their boss doesn't like them, thoughts that they messed up on a project last month and their coworker has it out for them and probably sabotaged them with the boss and instead of a raise they are going to get fired or demoted . . . Before long, this person cannot sleep or focus on anything else. Eating can be hard because their stomach is so upset from all the worry. See how unhealthy thoughts can transform into catastrophic thoughts that can cause unhealthy symptoms?

The same can happen when physical symptoms are felt in the body. Say you have a headache and instead of it being just a normal headache, you start thinking that it is a brain aneurysm or a tumor and you are going to die and what will happen to your family if you aren't there? Will your family lose everything and be left on the streets? These types of negative thoughts can spiral into full-blown panic if not stopped.

Checking the evidence can help you prevent those thoughts from getting out of control. With the first example of your annual review coming up, you can recognize when normal nervousness crosses the line into unhealthy stress and anxiety and then check the evidence. Does the evidence show that your boss doesn't like you or that she treats everyone the same as she treats you? Did you really mess up on the project last month? If you did mess up, was it really that bad and does it negate all the good things you have done for the company? In the second example above, if your head hurts do you have any evidence whatsoever for it being something more serious than a normal headache that everyone gets from time to time? Do you have any reason to make this headache into something serious enough to worry about?

When you check the evidence and get realistic about your anxious thoughts, more often than not you realize that your thoughts are over exaggerated. Use the evidence you find and replace unhealthy thinking with the appropriate and realistic thoughts that will help to manage your stress and anxiety.

#8
Be a Duck

I love this technique and use it myself on a regular basis. There is a saying about water rolling off a duck's back that I think most of us have heard. So, when something happens that would normally bother you, choose to be a duck. Let it roll right off of your back and don't let it stress you out.

If your teenager wants to argue with you about what she is wearing as you're trying to get out the door for school and work, be a duck and don't let it bother you as you let your child know that you are not allowing that outfit, but you love her anyway. Your mother-in-law passive-aggressively comments that your new haircut is not your best look. Don't get upset. Be a duck and let her comment roll right off your back as you remember how much you like your hair. Have a flat tire? Be a duck and don't stress about it as you call for help.

No matter what happens in your day and no matter what someone does or says to you, you get to choose how you react. Getting upset and stressing or worrying about it do not change it and will only make you feel worse. Things are easier to deal with if you stay calm while being a duck and handling whatever gets thrown at you.

#9
Learn to Manage Your Anger

Every one of us gets angry sometimes. Getting angry is not the problem. It is, after all, a normal, human emotion. It's what we do with that anger that can be the problem. Anytime we are having a big emotion such as anger or fear we are in the emotional part of our brain instead of our logical, thinking, calm brain. Learning to understand the cause of your anger as well as how to behave appropriately when you are angry are healthy ways to manage it and get you back into your calm brain faster.

When we are angry, we often say and do things we would never do if we were calm and in control. You might yell or call someone names that you later regret. You might hit or break something. When angry, you may hear things defensively and distort what was actually said. We might interpret others' motivations as malicious toward us when that couldn't be further from the truth.

Because anger can cause us to behave in ways we normally wouldn't, we should never discipline our children when we are angry, nor should we try to have in-depth discussions or make important decisions. As a parent, you should not try to talk to your children when they are in an angry state as they probably won't hear you anyway, because they are in their own emotional brain.

What you can do when angry is give yourself time to calm down. Grown-ups can give themselves a time-out just like they do kids. This gives you time to get out of your emotional brain and back into your logical, thinking brain so you can deal effectively and appropriately with whatever caused your anger in the first place.

Once you have calmed down and are back in your logical brain, stop and think about what triggered your anger. Anger is a secondary emotion and to manage it, you have to figure out what the primary emotion is that is feeding the anger. For example, if I get really angry at my husband, and I stop and think about why I am angry, I might find that my feelings were hurt. If I don't manage my anger appropriately, instead of addressing my hurt feelings, I could act out in anger toward him and say hurtful things I really don't mean.

It is often easier to feel anger than it is to acknowledge and feel the underlying emotions triggering the anger.

Hurt, embarrassment, and fear are just some of the emotions that feed anger and can be more difficult to acknowledge and deal with than anger, but if you don't deal with the primary emotions, the anger can get out of control. Anger can feel difficult to manage, but you can do it, and when you do it appropriately, you will feel much less stressed.

#10
Don't Compare

Have you ever caught yourself comparing your looks, your car, your job, your bank account, or other material things to what other people have? Of course you have. We all do that from time to time, but I strongly encourage you to catch yourself when you do it and stop it.

You will always be able to find someone who is smarter, wealthier, skinnier, faster, more successful, etc. And you know what? Who cares? There are people who also have less of whatever it is you are comparing than you do, too. Does that make you better than them if you have more than they do? Of course not! If you stop comparing and learn to be at peace with what you have and who you are, you will be so much happier.

You do not need to look outside of yourself to judge whether you are okay or not. There is nothing wrong with you the way you are. It doesn't matter if someone has more or less than you do. They are just different, and they are okay, too.

That does not mean that each of us should not look for ways we can improve, but make sure you are doing it for yourself. Do not let yourself get caught up doing it for others or to fit some kind of ridiculous mold of what you think you should be or should have. Let go of comparisons and enjoy what you have and who you are.

#11
Don't Be Afraid to Fail

One of the words I dislike most is *fail*. We cannot fail when we try something. What we try may not work out like we want it to, but with everything we try to do we learn something—even if it is what not to do again. We get to choose whether we take what we learn from our unsuccessful efforts and apply it to our lives for the better or whether to let it defeat us. There is no fail if you try. It is only a learning experience if we choose to let it be that way. And what is so scary about having a learning experience?

When something does not work out the way you had hoped and planned for, resist the urge to beat yourself up. It is not fair to do that to yourself. There is no such thing as a crystal ball that works to tell you the future. We have to try things and learn from what we tried so we can move on and be better than we could ever imagine. Sometimes that takes several learning experiences, but that's okay. If at first you don't succeed, try, try again. The only way to fail is to never try at all.

#12
Be Patient

I wish it were different, but patience is not one of my natural virtues. Nor is it for many people, especially when stressed. But the good news is that patience is a skill that can be developed with practice. Using this tool will help you decrease stress and anxiety on a daily basis.

We live in an instant gratification society where we want things right when we want them and strongly dislike having to wait. That's not a good thing because we cannot always immediately have our way. When we lose our patience, we experience several physical and mental stress reactions. Heart rate and blood pressure rise, muscles tense, we become irritable and can lash out at others. We can be viewed as entitled, arrogant, or insensitive when we behave impatiently, which is often exactly how we are acting. These reactions can make anxiety symptoms worse when we finally calm down and remember how we behaved in our impatience.

The next time you find yourself struggling to be patient, try this: First, take in a few deep belly breaths. As you breathe, imagine you are breathing in calm and blowing out frustration. Then use positive self-talk such as, "I can wait. The world will not stop spinning if I have to wait a few minutes."

If someone else is causing you to need patience, remember that not everyone has to move in your time. They are entitled to have their own way of doing things and are not required to do anything your way. You can calmly and politely ask them to do what you want, but accept that it may not happen.

Children and teens fit into this category, too. Be patient with them. They may be little people, but they still have their own way of doing things. You may have to wait a little longer for things to get done, but you can feel proud of yourself for being patient and know that your patience goes a long way toward building their self-esteem. You can do your breathing exercises to help you stay calm as you wait.

Remember this too: getting angry and stressed out in a situation you have no control over doesn't change the fact that you are going to have to wait anyway. You might as well stay calm while you wait instead of being stressed out. You will thank yourself later and leave others with a positive view of the good person you really are.

#13
Accept Change

Change can be very difficult to cope with, especially change we do not want. But change is also an unavoidable reality of life; fighting it is wasted energy. Instead, you can accept the change that is occurring. This does not mean that you have to be okay with the change or agree that it is for the best. You just have to accept that it is happening and take whatever lessons you can learn from it and use them to help you move on with your life.

Some changes are dramatic and life altering, such as a death or divorce. Some changes can be simpler such as starting a new job; moving to a new house, a new town, or a new school; or having to learn a new computer program. Some changes that cause stress are no more than getting to your favorite restaurant and finding out they no longer serve your favorite meal or realizing that roadwork causes you to have to take a new route home for a few weeks.

Any change, big or small, requires that you find a way to adapt and move on. When we fight against change or lament the way the change affects us, we suffer a lot of unnecessary stress and worry. The sooner you are able to find acceptance and adapt, the less likely you are to suffer.

#14
Have Good Boundaries

Boundaries are limits we set with the people in our lives, ourselves, and the world around us. Boundaries keep us safe both physically and mentally, help us to feel healthy, and ensure we are able to function as best we can.

A boundary may be not allowing your partner to be abusive, not allowing friends or bosses to take advantage of you, not lending money to someone, saying no when asked to do something you don't want to do, or making your children follow the rules you have set. Boundaries are how we allow people to treat us. When we have firm boundaries, it helps us to ensure that the people in our lives will treat us respectfully. Boundaries keep us safe emotionally and physically and help us to manage our stress.

We also need to set good boundaries with ourselves. Making sure we eat healthy and get enough sleep, using good conflict resolution skills, and having good self-care

are examples of personal boundaries we can set for ourselves.

Sometimes others do not like the boundaries we set, but when you set a boundary for something you need, others do not have to agree with you. Your boundaries are valid and necessary for you, and you do not need anyone else's permission to set a healthy boundary. It is not selfish to take care of yourself. There are some people who are toxic to your well-being, and they are the ones who will criticize you the most when your boundaries prevent them from getting what they want. That is all the more reason for you to set up strong boundaries to keep you healthy, happy, and much less stressed out.

#15
Let Go of the Past

The best way I know how to explain this technique is to compare it to driving a car. If you have a goal of getting from California to Maine, you have to keep your eyes on the road ahead of you while also paying attention to what is going on inside of the car, such as the gauges and pedals and so on, right? But, if you are driving in your car and only looking in the rear-view mirror, you will most certainly crash and will never arrive at your destination.

It is the same with how you live your life. If your goal is happiness and less stress, yet you only focus on the past you can see in your rear-view mirror, you will not be able to enjoy the present (what is going on inside of the car) or reach your destination (looking ahead).

It's true that you cannot ignore the past, but you cannot focus too much on it either. Deal with your past and come to terms with it. Learn what you can from it to help you reach your goals and enjoy the present, but do not let it consume you or you will crash and burn.

Focusing on the past can increase feelings of stress and anxiety and is wasted energy. No matter how much you focus on the past, you will not be able to change it. Do what you have control over, which is learning whatever lessons you can from the past, make peace with it, and use your experiences to make your life and the lives of those you love better now.

#16
Focus on the Positive

In times when you are feeling stressed and anxious, you will usually look for the negatives around you. It's not always a conscious thought. It's just that we look for things to support how we are feeling. It is called tracking. We tend to ignore the positives because we are not feeling positive and looking for positive things.

When my daughter learned how to play the slug bug game (finding Volkswagen Bug cars and pointing them out), I started seeing those cars everywhere. I was never looking for them before, but when the game started, we were all on the lookout for them every time we were in the car. The same amount of Volkswagens were out there whether or not I was looking for them, but I just hadn't seen them before we started playing the game. I was tracking them.

What this technique does is get you to start looking for the positives—your Volkswagen Bugs. The positive things are there if you just look for them. When you start looking for them you will see the positives everywhere. The negatives will decrease because you are no longer tracking them. You will find what you are looking for, so choose to look for the positives. Focus on what is right in your life and not what is wrong and you will begin to feel better.

#17
Not Everyone Has to Like You

It never feels good when we know someone does not like us, but the truth is that not everyone will like us. We each have our own preferences and personalities and we will not mesh well with everyone. That is okay.

What is important is that you do not base your self-worth on whether or not another person likes you. If you can look at yourself in the mirror and say that you like who you are and know that you do the best you can, what more can you ask of yourself?

It really is not important in the big scheme of things that some people do not like you. What is vitally important is that you like you. If there is something that you don't like about yourself, then you can take the necessary steps to change that. I have a plaque on the wall in my office that reads, "It's never too late to be who you want to be." I love that saying because it is so true. Be the person you want to be and love yourself for it. No one else's opinion matters as much as your own.

#18
Forgive

Sounds so easy, doesn't it? Just let it go and forgive. Well, you and I both know it isn't as simple as it sounds, but it is important. Holding on to a grudge against others hurts you so much more than it does the person who is the target of that grudge. To hold on to anger and resentment, you have to maintain some pretty negative and unhealthy thoughts against someone. Holding on to anger or hurt also keeps you a victim, which prevents you from healing.

Forgiving someone else begins with acknowledging your own part in the situation and forgiving yourself for that. Sometimes this step is more difficult than forgiving others. When you finally forgive yourself and release all of the negative emotions you hold in your body and mind, it is an amazingly freeing experience. You deserve that. Beating yourself up is very unfair, and it doesn't change anything; it only keeps you stuck in negativity and causes stress.

What if instead of holding on to a grudge against another person or yourself, you asked yourself what you have learned from the experience? There is always something we can learn in every situation. Take what you've learned, use it to help yourself grow, and move on. Let go of past hurts because you cannot change them. You have all the power in the world to make your life and the lives of those you love better. Holding on to anger never hurts the other person, but it always hurts us. Let it go. Forgive and be happy.

A powerful exercise that can help you forgive and let go is to write down what it is you are holding on to. Write about the incident, the people involved, what you think and feel about it. Describe your emotions in detail as well as how the incident has affected you. Then write down that you are choosing to forgive everyone involved. Take the paper and read it as many times as you feel you need to, then destroy it. You can tear it into a million pieces and flush it or burn it (safely, of course) and watch as it disappears. Finally, take in a deep breath, close your eyes, and visualize your heart feeling lighter and happier.

#19
Focus on What You Can Control

Have you ever noticed how much you focus on things you cannot possibly have any control over? That is such a waste of time and energy because it is a futile endeavor. We tend to worry about things like having an illness, something bad happening to someone we love, a partner cheating, someone talking badly about us, and on and on and on the list goes. If you think about it, you can't control any of those things.

Instead of worrying about something we cannot control, what if instead we focused on what we can do? Things like eating a healthy diet, getting enough exercise and sleep, and having positive, healthy thoughts to keep illness away?

Instead of worrying about something bad happening to a loved one, you can focus on making sure you love them and treat them well so you both feel good about the time you spend together. The same applies to fears of a partner cheating on you. If you bring your best to the relationship and have chosen your partner well, worrying about cheating does nothing to help strengthen the relationship and can, in fact, cause it to deteriorate.

Worrying about someone gossiping about you doesn't change what someone could say about you, but being a kind, responsible, and positive person helps to ensure others perceive you in a good way.

Worrying about what you have no control over is useless, but focusing on what you can control helps to ensure your fears are less likely to come true. You have so much more power than you know to make your life good.

#20
See the Best in Others

How many times have you become frustrated or hurt by someone because you assumed they had negative intentions? We can become so caught up in what we believe others think, feel, or mean by their actions that we let it cause us stress.

For example, if you think a coworker is giving you a dirty look, you might become angry and behave rudely back, take out your frustrations on someone else, or sit and worry all day about it. What if you chose to believe the best in your coworker instead? Imagine how much that would change your own emotions and behavior. Isn't it possible that person was thinking about something else and just happened to look your way? That it had nothing to do with you at all?

I have seen this as a common frustration among couples, too. Couples are really bad about believing they know what their partner thinks and means by their behavior. Oftentimes they are wrong. When something happens, instead of talking to each other, assumptions are made about motives, intentions, or hidden meanings. When the partners choose not to see the best in each other, they can retaliate in ways that are hurtful to the relationship. This behavior causes a problem where there may not have been one if they just chose to believe the best in each other.

When someone appears to have slighted you in some way, make the choice to believe this action was not malicious or intended. Change your assumption from something negative to something positive. One way you get upset and stressed out. The other way you feel pretty good.

#21
Talk Nicely to Yourself

Stop and think about how you talk to yourself. Is it kind and supportive or is it critical and negative? Often we are not very kind to ourselves. The way you talk to yourself has a huge impact on how you feel and act. If you notice that you are being judgmental and are always finding fault in yourself, criticizing every move you make, you're not going to feel strong and have a good self-image.

To change how you talk to yourself, you first have to become aware of what you are saying. When you catch yourself being negative, counter those thoughts with a realistic and positive one. Start talking to yourself like you would a friend. With your friends you show kindness, honesty, and support. You would never be critical or mean.

If you can catch yourself and replace negative self-talk with positive self-talk, you can improve your self-image and confidence. You might find that being supportive and nice to yourself allows you to extend that positive thinking to other situations in your life, which will only further improve your mental health and decrease stress.

#22
Let Go of Perfectionist Thinking

Did you know that there is no such thing as perfection? There is great, really awesome, and amazing, but no perfect. To beat yourself up for not achieving perfection is simply unfair. The best you can do is just that—your best.

I know that anxiety and stress can seriously hamper your efforts and even your motivation to do your best; however, if you are doing the best you can to manage your mental health, things will get better. The key is to put forth the best effort you can and don't stop trying, even when you find it is hard. And then give yourself some credit for all of your hard work.

There is one more thing about letting go of perfectionist thinking, and that is to realize that sometimes, good enough is okay—even wonderful. I have talked to so many people who do not allow themselves to enjoy their lives or their efforts because things do not measure up to what they think is perfect. They might do 95 percent of what they set out to accomplish, but only focus on the 5 percent they were unable to complete. What about giving credit for the 95 percent they did complete? It doesn't have to be perfect, great, really awesome, or amazing to be just fine. Good enough is good enough.

#23
Know the Difference between Helping and Being a Doormat

Sometimes our greatest strengths can also be a weakness for us. If you are a person who is loving, helpful, and compassionate and you try to help others in need, you might know where I'm going with this. If you don't know where to set the boundary between being helpful and being taken advantage of, you could find yourself being treated like a doormat. If you do this very long, it can cause a significant amount of stress and anxiety.

I do not wish to discourage anyone from being giving and kind, but I do wish to encourage you to set boundaries with yourself and others and to take care of your own needs first. Know when to say no as well as when to say yes.

Imagine you are a pitcher full of loving kindness and you are constantly filling everyone else's cups without taking care of yourself. Eventually, your pitcher will run dry and you will be of no help to anyone because you have exhausted your resources taking care of others. Good self-care and boundaries can ensure your pitcher stays full.

Another pitfall to watch out for is that there are many who will take advantage of your kindness. Unfortunately, there are those who will take and take without ever giving back to you in return. It is extremely important that you learn to set boundaries with these people. This does not make you a bad person who is selfish or mean, even though they may try to tell you this so you don't stop giving to them.

Helping must start with your helping yourself so you have more to give. You have a wonderful strength in your kindness and giving nature, but as with everything in life, there must be a balance for it to be healthy.

#24
Don't Avoid

Avoidance is a huge factor in stress and anxiety. It makes sense that we avoid what we don't want to do and what we don't want to feel, think about, or remember. Chronic avoidance, though, can increase stress and anxiety to very unhealthy levels. We must find a way to face what we avoid because that is the only way to effectively manage what we fear.

When we avoid things, we do not deal with them; if we don't deal with them, they can get bigger. Just like a wound that is not properly treated becomes infected, what we avoid can begin to fester within us. Dealing with the things we avoid is like medicating that wound and allowing it to heal. There may still be a scar, but it doesn't stop us from living life.

Another way to think of avoidance is that what we are avoiding is always coloring the lens through which we view the world. It is always there affecting everything we see. When you stop avoiding it, you look at it head-on and can truly process everything about it, and then you are able to put it away. It no longer affects everything you see because it is not in your line of sight. It is still part of your story but no longer your identity, and it stops affecting your everyday life.

Avoidance is a short-term solution that never helps in the long run and almost always makes that which we are avoiding more of a problem for us. Stop avoiding and learn to cope with the difficult emotions and feelings that come up when you face your fears. Using healthy coping skills and taking small, consistent steps toward your goal will help you achieve the peace and calm you are looking for.

#25
Let Go of Control

Control in life and controlling others are illusions. Control is not real. For those who are highly anxious, that illusion of control tricks them into feeling like they can manage their lives by telling themselves that if they work harder to get control, they will feel better. They work and work to try to attain something they will never have. Talk about stressful!

To help you let go of this illusion, you can start by acknowledging that the only thing you have control over is yourself. You can control your thoughts and behaviors, and by taking control of those, you can manage your emotions. That's it. That is the extent of what you can ever control.

You have no control over what others do or what is going to happen. The best you can do is work to set up your life so that you can manage as best you can what goes on in it, but ultimately you have no control over anything else.

Trying to control everyone and everything around us is ultimately rooted in fear. It is a fear that if we don't control everything, something bad could happen. That fear and the efforts expended to control take up a lot of energy and sabotage a lot of happiness. Instead, what if you let go of trying to control and trust that you have done a good job of managing your life? What if you could trust that all will be okay and as it should be? Can you imagine how much more peaceful and less stressed you would be? The truth is, whether you let go or not, what is going to happen will happen. So let go and free up your energy so you can enjoy your life.

#26
Pick Your Battles

Conflict is stressful for everyone—even for people who are good at handling conflict. We are faced with conflict nearly every day in families, at work, shopping, driving, with friends, and at school. Some confrontations are necessary, but it is important to choose which battles are worth fighting.

In my work with families in particular, I try to help parents and children identify when to engage in conflict and when it just isn't worth it. As parents, we often want our children to be perfect and just listen to whatever we tell them without question, but that is not realistic or healthy. Children will often fight for their independence, to get their way and act out their feelings in a safe place at home. When children push back, I encourage parents to stop and take a breath and choose whether it is worth fighting with their children over. Is this a good time for their children to learn a valuable lesson, or to just feel like they have a win?

The same applies to other types of conflicts whether it is with your spouse, boss, coworker, friend, teacher, or even the rude cashier at the checkout—you have to ask yourself if this is a battle worth fighting. Is it worth the stress, anxiety, and the possible consequences it could cause? Many times the person you are fighting with is going through something that is causing them to behave the way they are. Do you really need to add to it by engaging in conflict? You also have to think about what you would really win if you engaged. Some issues are worth fighting for, but there are a lot more that just aren't worth it. Most often, walking away makes you the real winner.

#27
Use Fair Fighting Skills

When you find yourself in a situation in which you need to engage in conflict (and sometimes you will), using positive conflict resolution skills can help to manage and decrease the stress and anxiety of the situation.

Positive conflict resolution skills, or as I like to call them, fair fighting skills, are pretty simple. In a conflict, you state what you want or need respectfully, you state how you are feeling, and, if appropriate, you state why you feel that way. There is no blaming, name-calling, intimidating, yelling, or manipulating, and you stick to the subject at hand.

You also need to fully listen to the other person's side of the conflict, be respectful of their feelings, and reasonably consider their point of view. In conflict, we often listen defensively and do not truly hear what the other person is saying. We assume we know what the other person is going to say or we dismiss what the other person is saying because we think we know what they really mean. When you are listening for their point of view, one way to ensure you are hearing what the other person is actually saying is to reflect back what you understand them to be saying. Say something like, "I hear you say x, y, and z. Is this correct?"

Positive conflict resolution also requires that you let go of the need to win. Focus instead on how you can both find a way to emerge from the conflict feeling good. Finding a way that both of you can come out of the conflict feeling it was handled fairly would be a win-win for both sides and go a long way toward decreasing negative feelings for both of you.

#28
Look for Exit Ramps

When you find yourself in a situation where you are beginning to feel stressed, look for an exit ramp to get off the stress highway. Exit ramps allow you to change, stop, or at least be able to get away from a negative situation so you are no longer a participant. Exit ramps are not always easy to spot, but there is usually always something you can do (or not do) that can help you in the situation.

Sometimes when I talk to people about this tool, they feel like there are exit ramps available, but using those strategies lets the other person win. My response to that is that you are trying to manage your stress and anxiety, so the biggest winner when you take an exit ramp is you. For example, if you and your girlfriend are talking and find that the conversation is heading into a hot button topic, you can simply change the subject or tell her that she has an interesting point of view and you will have to think about it. You are not saying you agree with her, you are not engaging in a debate with her or letting her win at all. Your exit ramp helped you to avoid a potential fight and all the stress that would come with the confrontation.

It doesn't matter how others look at your exit ramp, it matters that it works for you. Finding your exit ramps is a very effective tool in managing stress and anxiety both during a potentially difficult situation as well as in your overall life.

#29
Find Your But

Stress, anxiety, and worry are not positive emotions, nor do they lead to positive thoughts. In fact, being stressed or anxious increases the likelihood that you will have negative thoughts on a regular basis.

One of the tools that can help manage negative thinking is to find your "but." No, I do not mean your bottom. What I do mean is that when you find yourself thinking negative thoughts, change them into positive thoughts by using "but."

If you find working with a particular coworker is stressful, challenge that negative thought by saying, "*But*, at least I have a job." If you think your children's fighting is driving you crazy, say to yourself, "*But*, I am thankful I have those beautiful kids." If you have to present your paper at school and you are very nervous about it, think to yourself, "*But*, I know everyone presenting will be nervous, too." You may be really frustrated with your partner, "*But*, I really do love him/her."

No matter what negative thought you are having, you can always find a "but." Intentionally choosing to think positive thoughts can greatly reduce the stress and anxiety that negativity causes.

#30
Take Charge of Your
Own Happiness

We've all heard the saying that happiness comes from within, but I think it is easy to forget that sometimes. We give others the responsibility for our happiness, which is very unfair as well as unrealistic. Putting your emotional well-being in the hands of anyone else is incredibly stressful and anxiety-provoking for you as well as the person who is in charge of your happiness.

When you decide to take charge of your happiness, you have the opportunity to step into your own power. What do you want out of life? What do you want out of yourself? Those are actually big questions so give yourself time to really think about the answers. Maybe even journal about what your ideal life would look like. Once you figure that out, you can see where you need to make some changes. You can also see where things are going well and what you might need to continue to do more of! You are in charge of your life and are the only one on this planet who can make you happy.

#31
Accept Yourself

It feels horrible when the people who are supposed to love you want to change you. The message that is sent is that you are not good enough. It hurts even worse when you won't accept yourself. The truth is that you are good enough and that acceptance has to start with you.

We are all born with personality traits and inherent talents. Those traits and talents are sculpted over time by our life experiences and the people we are surrounded by. If you feel like you've been working against the current of who you really are inside, always trying to ignore your wants and desires in favor of what you think you are "supposed" to be, that is pretty stressful.

I recently found a quote by Albert Einstein who said, "Everybody is a genius. But if you judge a fish by its ability to climb a tree, it will live its whole life believing that it is stupid." This quote eloquently illustrates my point, and is one of my new favorites.

What do you think it would feel like if you stopped trying to be something you are not and embraced who you really are? I don't believe that the Divine Creator makes mistakes, and no mistakes were made when you were born. You are special and unique and you should let go and be who you were made to be.

#32
Know Your Triggers

Self-awareness is a very important tool in managing stress and anxiety. This includes knowing what triggers you to feel stressed or anxious. H.A.L.T. is an acronym that many therapists use to help their clients know when to take steps toward managing their stress because everyone is triggered when facing these common stressors. H.A.L.T. stands for Hungry, Angry, Lonely, and Tired.

But we all have our own personal triggers, too. Perhaps taking on too much at work, procrastinating, and being around certain people or situations are triggers for you. When you know what triggers you, you can take steps to mitigate that trigger's power to hurt you.

When identifying your triggers, be very careful not to say to yourself that you should be able to handle this stressor or criticize yourself in any way for your triggers. There are no "shoulds" when it comes to stressors. If it bothers you, it bothers you and that is okay. Once you know and accept this, you can take steps toward managing it.

Steps can include things like eating at regular intervals so your blood sugar is stable and you won't feel hungry, getting enough sleep the night before a day when you know you will be busy, or having a plan for self-care when you have had a stressful day. When you know what triggers you, that gives you power to manage your triggers and stay in control of your emotions.

#33
Eustress vs. Distress

You might not know that there are two types of stress: eustress and distress. We're all pretty familiar with distress—the negative situations or events that increase feelings of stress and being overwhelmed. Eustress is a type of stress associated with positive events and situations that we don't really think of as dis-stressful, but this type of stress is just as demanding on the body and mind as distress.

Eustress can occur when one is planning a wedding, buying a new house, starting school, having a baby, or interviewing for a job. These are all good events in your life, but still stressful.

Regardless of something being eustress or distress, your body reacts the same way because both are stress. Remember that stress is caused by anything that places a demand on the body. So just because an event is good, don't forget that it can still stress you out—you need to take self-care steps to deal effectively with eustress, too.

#34
Think Before You Speak

We are all guilty of saying something we later regret or kicking ourselves later for what we wished we would have said. The purpose of this technique is to encourage you to learn to think before you speak. Self-control and self-regulation around what we say are paramount to having successful relationships with less stress and anxiety.

For those who stress and worry a lot, ruminating (having the same thoughts over and over) on what they wished they would have said or what they regret saying is a big problem. Whether it stems from a confrontation you had, a missed opportunity to express yourself in a conversation, or regret about spouting off without thinking, worrying about how we communicated in the past can cause a lot of stress.

One way you can avoid this situation is to give yourself a moment to take a deep, calming breath before speaking so you can gather your thoughts. If you find that you need a little more time, you can tell the other person that you would like to talk to them about this issue, but need some time to think about it before you do. You don't have to feel pressured to complete a conversation all at once when you aren't ready.

It is also a good idea to mentally rehearse what you want to say if you know beforehand that there will be a discussion. It can feel silly, but really imagine that this conversation is occurring. Imagine what you will say and what you think the other person will say. Imagine yourself handling the situation in a mature, appropriate way that leaves you feeling good about yourself. If you have questions, talk to someone in your support system who you know will have good advice to help you prepare.

If you have taken the time to choose your words and to say those words in an appropriate way, you will have much less to worry about. You won't have to beat yourself up for saying something you wish you wouldn't have said or regretted the way you said it. You will have eliminated something that would have normally been stressful because you were ready.

#35
Know Where You Are on the Escalation Scale

0..5..10
No Stress   Most Possible Stress

Knowing your position on the escalation scale gives you a lot of power in controlling stress and anxiety. Imagine that 0 represents no stress at all and 10 represents the most stressed you can be. You want to try to keep your baseline under 3 on a daily basis. For sure you need to be below a 5 when having serious discussions, making important decisions, and disciplining your children.

When you are above a 5, you are in the emotional part of your brain—the place where we are when we are in fight, flight, or freeze mode. That's where we are when we have big emotions such as anger and fear. When we are in our emotional brain, we are much more likely to say and do things we shouldn't and we are probably not going to be able to hear exactly what is being said to us because we are hearing it through a high-emotion filter, which often distorts the message. As parents, we should NEVER discipline our children when we are above a 5, nor should we expect our children to hear us as we try to get them to understand why they are in trouble if they are above a 5.

You might be wondering how to know where you are on the escalation scale. The answer is to look within. Take inventory of how your body feels when it is below a 5. You are more relaxed. Your heart rate and blood pressure are normal; you can take slow, deep breaths. Your body doesn't feel tense. Think about where you feel stress in your body. Is it in your stomach, shoulders, or neck? Maybe you notice your jaw or fists clench. Becoming aware of how tension and stress affect you can give you a clue as to where you are on the scale.

The rule I have for myself and encourage my clients to adopt is that if you recognize you are escalating on the scale and have reached a 5, know that is the time to zip your lips and take a time-out. While you are taking a break, do some deep breathing, take a walk, talk to a friend, or try any number of the techniques in this book. Doing these things can help you relax and get back under a 5 so you are in a more positive emotional position to continue.

An important thing to remember about the escalation scale is that it is much easier to go from a 5 down to a 2 or 3 than it is to go from 10 down to 8. The higher you are on the scale, the more time you should allow yourself to get back into your relaxed state.

#36
Be Aware (and Beware) of Secondary Stress

Secondary stress, also known as secondary traumatic stress and compassion fatigue, is a unique type of stress that those who work with survivors of a primary trauma endure. For example, social workers who work with abused children can develop secondary stress from being exposed to the children's abuse. The same can be true for first responders, therapists, doctors and nurses, journalists, veterans, and anyone else who is exposed to other people's suffering. Just listening to another person's story of trauma or witnessing firsthand the after effects of a trauma such as what a police officer may see at the scene of a shooting or car accident can be enough to trigger secondary traumatic stress symptoms.

Be aware of the signs of secondary stress, which include poor concentration, sadness, fatigue, physical illness, nightmares, and anger. If you are in a situation where you are exposed to other people's traumas and notice that you are thinking, feeling, or behaving in ways that are concerning to you, take action right away. Talk with your supervisor, therapist, or anyone else in your support system about what is going on, develop a strong stress management routine, and practice some of the techniques in this book. In extreme circumstances, you may need to evaluate whether or not you should continue in your position.

Do not dismiss your own secondary stress. I have heard people say things like, "It didn't happen to me so what am I complaining about?" I try to help them see that it is not unusual or wrong that they are experiencing secondary stress. It is normal and they are entitled to their feelings. Ignoring or stuffing those feelings can cause other problems. See tip #38 to see what I mean.

#37
Deal with Your Past

It's very easy to try to forget the past when your past has been traumatic or difficult. Seriously, who wants to think about times that were hard and stressful? Unfortunately, though, if you haven't dealt with your past, you can only bury or stuff it for so long before it pops up somewhere in your life.

Unresolved issues from your past can show up as anxiety or depression (sometimes both); a physical illness; something that affects your sleep, eating habits, your view of the world and people; and in other behaviors and emotions that are unhealthy. Unresolved issues often color your entire view of the world and negatively impact your quality of life.

When you decide to deal with your past, you can process it in a way that allows you to look at it, find a way to resolve it, and put it away so that it no longer affects your daily life. You cannot change that it is part of your story, but when you deal with it, it is no longer part of your identity. You take away its power to affect your life.

Working with a qualified therapist is the most effective way to process and deal with your past. I cannot promise you that this will be easy; it will likely be pretty hard and emotional at times. But, what I can assure you is that it is worth it. There is no such thing as a quick fix or magic pill in dealing with the past. You have to do the work, but you can do it and you will come out on the other side of it much healthier and happier and stronger.

#38
Acknowledge Your Feelings

Feelings can be hard sometimes, especially feelings such as anger, sadness, hurt, embarrassment, and vulnerability. It may seem like it is easier to avoid these feelings, ignore them, or stuff them down than to deal with them, but our body and our mind have a way of forcing us to deal with our emotions. Sometimes they can come out in different ways such as by affecting your mental or physical health or showing up as emotions that seem easier or feel safer to feel such as anger.

Anger is a secondary emotion and can be easier to feel than the primary emotions that are feeding the anger. For instance, many people who are going through a divorce get stuck in anger at their ex rather than dealing with the primary emotions of hurt, embarrassment, or feelings of abandonment that are actually driving their anger. They can feel righteous and stronger in their anger rather than accept the vulnerability of processing what they are truly feeling underneath that anger. Getting stuck in that anger often causes a lot of unnecessary pain and trauma to everyone involved, especially their children, who are stuck in the middle of that divorce.

I hear a lot of "I should" or "I shouldn't" be feeling this way and other judgmental statements when people talk about what they are feeling. Feelings and emotions are not always logical, and it is not wrong to have whatever feelings you are having. Acknowledge your feelings and deal with what they are. It will decrease stress when you take the judgment out of your acknowledgement and simply accept that what you feel is okay for you as you learn how to cope with them.

One final thing to say about this tool is that you do not need anyone's permission or agreement to have your feelings. I've had people tell me that others have told them they are being ridiculous, stupid, or somehow inappropriate for their feelings. Admittedly it feels good when we are validated, but you do not need this. Your feelings are your own and how you feel is just fine. The important thing is that you take responsibility for your emotions and find ways to effectively cope with however you are feeling so that you can be happy.

#39
Play the Odds with Worry

Oftentimes people will worry and stress over things that are not likely to happen. We can spend a huge majority of our day and night getting ourselves all worked up and worrying about future events that are very unlikely to ever happen.

When working with people who are stressed or anxious about something, I will ask them what the chances are of this event actually happening. After considering all of the facts, most will say that there is less than a 10 percent chance of it happening. In truth, most of the time the likelihood of their fears actually happening are under 5 percent, but many will spend 90 percent of their time and

51

energy worrying about something that has a 5 percent or less chance of occurring. That is a lot of wasted energy!

How different would their life be if they chose to focus on the more than 90 percent chance that all will be okay? If this sounds like you, what could you do with all of that extra time and energy? You can prepare as best you can for what you're concerned about, but don't waste your precious resources on worrying about what is highly unlikely to happen.

#40
Have Reasonable Goals

We all have goals we want to accomplish for ourselves, our families and friends, our communities, and our jobs. What we have to be careful of is making sure that the goals we set are realistic and the time we give ourselves to achieve these goals is manageable. Be careful not to take on too much.

Imagine the person who tries to take on the world never saying no to anyone or any task that requires a volunteer. That person doesn't have the resources to do everything all at once with any reasonable expectation of doing things well and still taking care of their own needs. No one could.

Only commit to doing what is best for you and your family. That's what should matter most to you. You cannot take care of the world and do everything. It is not selfish to have limits, and when you set healthy ones, you will have the time, energy, and focus to complete what you choose to take on and do it well.

When you are setting goals, think of long-term goals as well as short-term goals you can achieve quickly. Prioritize them according to what is best for your life. Break down long-term goals into short-term, easily doable goals. Not only does this help you stay focused and on task, it also helps to motivate you to continue on to reach your ultimate goal every time you achieve the smaller goals. Do not get down on yourself or let others criticize you for managing your goals the way that is best for you. As long as you are moving in the right direction and feel good about your progress, you are doing just fine.

#41
Focus on the Present

I talked a little about this technique in #15 Let Go of the Past, but I want to expand the concept a bit here. Focusing on the past or obsessing about the future will prevent you from giving the present the attention it requires to help you live a happy and healthy life.

Just like you cannot successfully drive a car while only looking in the rear-view mirror, you cannot successfully drive a car without paying attention to what is going on in the car and on the road around you. You have to monitor your gauges to make sure everything is working well in your vehicle, take care of the passengers in your car, monitor your speed, and pay attention to the road you are currently driving on.

Focusing on the present allows you to enjoy your life and all that is going on in it. You get to appreciate who you are now, not who you might be in the future or who you were in the past. It is a really freeing experience to give yourself permission to enjoy exactly what is going on in this moment of your life.

Mindfulness is an effective practice that helps you learn to be present and focus on the here and now. It helps you learn to notice your thoughts and feelings without judgment as they happen. This technique teaches you to pay attention to your thoughts and manage the emotional responses to them, which helps to decrease stress and anxiety.

#42
Don't Sabotage Yourself

While this may seem like a no-brainer to some, self-sabotaging behavior is more common than you might think. Sometimes this behavior can be obvious, like messing up a job because deep down you don't think you deserve it. Sometimes it can be less obvious, such as procrastinating or breaking off a relationship with someone who was really good for you because you kept finding fault in the littlest things.

Self-sabotaging behavior comes from a variety of sources. Oftentimes it's that you do not feel like you deserve good things because of low self-esteem. Some people come from families where all of their role models demonstrated self-sabotaging behavior so that is what they think is normal. It can also come from a place of fear. If you worry that something is too good and you are afraid it will somehow end, you might do something that ends it on purpose so you are the one in charge of ending it rather than risk the hurt of something else causing it to end.

Take a moment to evaluate your own behavior and notice if there is any self-sabotaging going on with you. If you find any, evaluate where this is coming from and take the necessary steps to stop that behavior and consciously engage in behavior that will lead you to the happiness you deserve.

#43
Boost Your Self-Esteem

If I asked you to tell me what is wrong with you, I would be willing to bet that you can come up with several things right off the top of your head. But, if I were to ask you what is right with you, would the answers come as easily? For many, that is much harder to do. We are almost always more critical of ourselves than anyone else would ever be. We would never talk to others the way we talk to ourselves because it would be unkind and hurtful. So why do it to yourself?

Notice your thoughts and begin to identify all the mean things you say to yourself. Every time you catch yourself saying something that is unkind, stop yourself and intentionally find something kind to say to yourself. If you find it difficult to think of something nice to say, think about some of the kind things that others have said to you and use one of those. My guess is that you have a ton of good things about you, and if you would just acknowledge them, your self-esteem would increase to a healthier and more accurate level.

There are other things you can do to boost your self-esteem. One is to find some activities that you enjoy and feel you are good at. Regularly engaging in an activity you find fun while at the same time increasing your skill level builds self-esteem.

Finishing a task you have been putting off, being kind to others, honoring your own likes and dislikes, setting healthy boundaries, and any other activity that you feel is healthy and good for you will also help to increase your self-esteem.

An exercise that might help you is to take a piece of paper and write down all the things you would have to be to finally be good enough for yourself. Write down what you would have to change. Make sure it is realistic. Talk about your list with loved ones to get their input on it. Oftentimes when I do this exercise with clients, they find that they are pretty great already. They also find that a lot of the traits they think they need, they already have. They just don't give themselves credit for their good qualities because they don't pay attention to them. If you can identify things you want to improve (like everyone on the planet can), taking steps toward achieving those goals will also help to boost your self-image.

#44
Don't Overreact

When we are feeling stressed out or anxious, it is very easy to overreact to things that happen. Our overreactions can cause problems for us that can further increase the negative feelings we are already experiencing.

To help prevent overreacting, first you have to recognize when you are doing it. Once you can recognize this, you can take steps to stop it. One thing I try to do that is very effective for me is, when something happens and I notice I have an immediate emotional and even physical reaction to it, I try to stop and think about why I am having this reaction and what might be fueling this reaction within me. If someone else is involved, I try to ask myself what that person is also going through before I react. Just those few seconds to stop and think have been helpful in preventing me from overreacting on more than one occasion. No one is perfect (least of all me) so if you do overreact, you should apologize and try to make amends.

There are quite a few techniques in this book that can help you manage your emotions and behaviors when you feel yourself beginning to escalate. You can also ask someone you trust to help you by letting you know if your reactions are appropriate and to give you advice on how to handle things when they come up. If you find you have overreacted and this affected someone else, it is not too late to make amends. Take what you learned and use it to help you next time something happens.

Things You Can Do to Conquer Anxiety & Stress

#45
Practice Relaxation Breathing

Did you know that when you are stressed or feeling anxious you actually breathe differently? It's true. When you're stressed, you typically take short, shallow breaths using your shoulders rather than your diaphragm to bring air into your lungs. This type of breathing can exacerbate the physical symptoms of stress and anxiety such as lightheadedness, heart palpitations, tightness/heaviness in the chest, and that tingling sensation often felt during a panic attack. This type of breathing is triggered by your body's sympathetic nervous system, which is in control when you are feeling stressed, anxious, or angry.

Your sympathetic nervous system starts releasing stress hormones that are working to get your nervous system back in parasympathetic control, which is your body's relaxed state. To help trigger your parasympathetic nervous system, you can intentionally take in slow, deep breaths. Take a few minutes just to breathe as deeply as feels comfortable to you and allow your breath to go down deep into your belly (diaphragmatic breaths). You should be able to feel your hand moving on your stomach when you breathe in if you are doing diaphragmatic breathing properly.

Another way to breathe for relaxation is to count as you breathe in and out. Just count to a number that feels good to you as you breathe in and then try to count to that same number as you breathe out. Try to focus on nothing but the air coming in and exiting through your nose or mouth, and let all stressful thoughts drift away.

One more breathing technique is to imagine that as you are breathing in, you are breathing in air that is the color of relaxation. It can be any color that represents a sense of peaceful, calm relaxation to you. Imagine that this color of relaxation surrounds your entire body like a bubble and the color is spreading throughout your body from head to toe as you breathe the color in slowly and deeply. If you are feeling tension in your body, imagine that color deepening where you are feeling tense and relaxing away the stress in those muscles. Imagine that deeper color of relaxation is melting away the tension as you continue to breathe deeply and slowly.

Give yourself at least five to ten minutes to use relaxation breathing anytime you feel you need to, but even taking relaxing breaths for shorter amounts of time can be beneficial. I really like this technique because it is something that you can do anytime and anywhere and no one will know what you are doing. Relaxation breathing is the first behavioral tool I teach my clients because it is easy to do, can be done anywhere without anyone knowing what you are doing, and it is very effective in helping you to get your body and mind into a relaxed state.

#46
Manage or Eliminate Unhealthy Relationships

Relationships can be tricky things. We have romantic partners, friends, neighbors, parents, siblings, teachers, bosses, coworkers, children, and acquaintances and each of these relationships has the potential to be good or bad. Most all of us have found ourselves in an unhealthy relationship at some time in our lives. We have to learn to either eliminate or manage these relationships or they can become toxic to us.

So what constitutes an unhealthy relationship? The most obvious type of unhealthy relationship is a relationship in which you are put down, used, abused, dominated, or controlled. It is never, ever okay for anyone to treat you badly, but this is especially true for those people in your life who are supposed to love you.

Unhealthy relationships can also occur when you are the only person in the relationship who is contributing. Instead of a give and take relationship, you are the only one giving and never getting anything in return. The people in these types of relationships typically want you to listen to them, but they don't have the time to listen to you. They want you to help them, but are conveniently never available to help when you need it.

If you find you are in an unhealthy relationship, you have two choices. You either need to end it or find a way to manage it so you are safe emotionally and physically. Ending toxic relationships is not always easy, especially if there is an emotional component to the relationship such

63

as one with a family member or a spouse. For those types of relationship, you have to ask yourself if you would be happier and healthier if that relationship were to end. This is not an easy decision that is made lightly; it requires a lot of thought and soul searching, but if your answer is yes, then you should let that relationship go for your best good. It is not selfish, mean, or cold-hearted to end toxic, unhealthy relationships. It is, in fact, a kind and healthy step for yourself.

If, after some deep consideration, your answer is no or that you are not sure, don't end that relationship just yet and evaluate whether you can find a way to manage that relationship. You have to find ways to continue that relationship while also staying safe. I use an analogy with my clients that seems to put things into perspective: If you have a snake in your home, you keep it in a cage, and you do not stick your hand into that cage because you know it will bite you, because it's a snake and that's what snakes do. You may feel you can't get rid of the snake so you have to feed it and take care of it. To keep the snake, you have to learn to interact with the snake in a healthy way so that you stay safe without sticking your hand in the cage.

An example would be if you have a toxic relationship with your parent (the snake) but do not feel you should end that relationship. You need to find a way to maintain that relationship with your parent while staying safe. So, if you have to go and visit for some reason (potential for biting), you would stay in a hotel instead of at their home. So that your parent cannot hurt you, you set yourself up by limiting your time with them and having a place you can escape to if needed. You wouldn't want to do things like accept money from your parents because you know it could lead to controlling behavior by them (biting).

Toxic people often try to make you feel guilty for setting boundaries with them—like you are the bad one for not letting them be abusive to you! Love yourself enough to set those boundaries because toxic relationships cause a lot of stress and anxiety and you deserve better.

#47
Be Assertive, Not Aggressive

There is a big difference between being assertive and being aggressive though many people do not understand the difference. This lack of understanding can cause a lot of problems as most people do not respond well to anyone who is being aggressive to them.

I think of assertive and aggressive as two opposite ends of a spectrum. Behaviors on the assertive end of the scale allow you to stand up for yourself or something you feel is important while using healthy communication skills. The behaviors on the aggressive end of the scale include crossing another person's personal boundaries in your attempt to get what you want.

Being assertive means you can feel good about making sure your needs are met without infringing on anyone else's needs. To be assertive you need to clearly communicate to the other party what you want without blaming, name-calling, yelling, bullying, manipulating, or in any other way being inappropriate. Aggressive communication is just the opposite and can manifest in different ways.

One type of aggressive communication is to demand, intimidate, yell, or bully without regard for how your behavior affects the other person because you want what you want. This kind of aggressive communicator can justify their behavior and will minimize the effects their communication style has on others.

Another type of aggressive communication occurs with people who are not used to asking for what they want or standing up for themselves. Often, when they try to be assertive, they go way overboard and become aggressive. This type of aggressiveness doesn't come from a sense of entitlement. Instead, it comes from a lack of knowing how to be assertive combined with nervous anxiety and a fear of confrontation that prevent them from saying what they really want to say in an appropriate way.

Fortunately, assertiveness is a skill that can be learned. There are tons of books and websites on the subject and I encourage you to check them out. Another way to learn the skill is to start paying attention to the people around you who communicate assertively and watch how they do it. You might even learn from people on television or in movies whom you admire for their ability to be assertive and get what they want. Once you've learned a few ways to be assertive, practice what you've learned in your new life and see how much easier it is when you know a confrontation is coming. You will know how to stand up for yourself and have a better chance to get what you want with much less stress.

#48
Walk Away

One of the hardest things to do sometimes is to walk away. This is especially true if you feel justified in whatever it is you are fighting for. But, if you gave yourself a moment to step back and evaluate whether continuing to fight is worth it, what the pros and cons of continuing are, you might be surprised at your conclusion.

If the only answer you can come up with is that you are fighting for your pride or to make a point—just to win—I would ask you again to reevaluate. Stop and think about why it matters so much to you that this other person agrees with you. In most cases, I would be willing to bet that it doesn't really matter at all.

The consequences of not walking away can be significant. Stress is most certainly one of the consequences, but what else is a consequence for you? Strained relationships, poor work environment, and anger are just a few. So you have to really consider whether walking away is the best solution.

Imagine what life could be like if you were able to just walk away from unnecessary conflict. Just let things roll off of your back like a duck (#8). Would you feel less stressed? We both know the answer to that question is a resounding "YES!"

#49
Say I'm Sorry

Holding on to guilt and shame for something you feel you were wrong about can cause a lot of stress and anxiety. The same is true if someone else thinks you did something wrong and wants an apology from you. Even if you don't think you were wrong, in that situation, you have to decide if apologizing is a good option to repair that relationship and reduce stress.

Saying you are sorry can be very difficult. Acknowledging you made a mistake can make you feel embarrassed and vulnerable. It also sets you up for the possibility that the person you are apologizing to might reject your apology. Neither scenario feels good.

For some people, their pride won't allow them to admit they are wrong and they fear appearing weak. Others feel that if they do not apologize, they do not have to take responsibility for their actions. Not accepting responsibility and apologizing when you are wrong demonstrates weak character, a lack of insight, and a disregard for others' feelings. Most people do not intentionally want to behave this way, and when they do, they feel an enormous amount of stress. How much lighter would that person feel if they just let go and said they were sorry when they were wrong?

Saying you are sorry can be the most freeing, healthy thing you can do sometimes. Being accountable to yourself and to the one you wronged shows a tremendous amount of strength and character. It can help you let go of the past and move on. Most of the time, saying you are sorry helps the other person and your relationship, but the best part is what it can do for you. Allow yourself to apologize and free yourself from the chains holding you back from your happiness.

#50
Indulge in Guilty Pleasures

Do you have something that you enjoy that others would say is ridiculous or a waste of time? I do. My family makes fun of me for a certain reality show I love to watch. And you know what? I don't care. I love watching this show and I watch it every time it is on. I record it, too, so I can see it if I miss it and even go back and re-watch it sometimes. A waste of time? Kind of. Watching this show does nothing to improve me as a human, nor does its being on the air do anything for the world, but I still like it.

Indulging in this guilty pleasure does one thing, though. It is my time to check out and just enjoy the program. I like it, and it reduces my stress. So I guess it does do something positive for me that my family just doesn't get.

I have a friend whose guilty pleasure is to have a piece of dark chocolate candy after every meal. She doesn't feel guilty about it or care what anyone thinks about it. It makes her happy. If you have something that you enjoy doing and it doesn't hurt you or anyone else, I say go for it. Indulge yourself, but do it within reason, of course.

There are some who cannot indulge their guilty pleasures within appropriate boundaries and they can quickly become unhealthy behaviors. If your guilty pleasure affects any area of your life—finances, relationships, health, etc., then I would strongly caution you against participating. A guilty pleasure that is healthy and a stress reliever does not in any way hurt anyone or anything in your life.

#51
Find a Hobby

Life these days can be incredibly busy so the idea of incorporating a hobby into your life might sound a little daunting. You don't have to spend hours per day or week on a hobby, but it can be a huge stress reliever to engage in an activity you enjoy.

I've never been a crafty person, but my daughter learned to crochet and wanted to teach me. I went along with it because I thought it would be a bonding activity we could do together, but I have to say I am hooked (no pun intended). I don't think anyone would ever call me an expert or even remotely good, but it is something I can do that helps to relax my body and my mind. We do it together some evenings as we watch television or a movie, and sometimes I do it alone.

You don't have to do something crafty like I did, but I do encourage you to find something you find relaxing and fun. It is preferable to find an activity that you can do often and fits in easily with your life. A hobby you can do with a friend or family member you like to spend time with is a bonus.

Hobbies are great stress relievers. They are also a very healthy coping mechanism to utilize when feeling depressed or when your anxiety is high. It can take your mind off of unhealthy thoughts, and can be a great distraction when you need one.

#52
Reach Out and Accept Help

Recognizing that you do not have to do everything alone is the first step in getting help. Too often we think we have to take care of everything ourselves and feel like we have somehow failed if we find we could use a little assistance. It is not a failure to realize you need some help. In fact, it is a huge strength to be able to acknowledge our limits.

Once you recognize you need help, the next step is asking for it. Many worry that friends or family do not have the time or energy to help, and feel bad asking. Some feel awkward and fear that others will look down on them for needing help or think they are a bother.

Just remember that you are important. Those who love you recognize this and you must recognize it in yourself and ask for help when you need it. You might be surprised at how much help is available if you would only ask.

The other problem with getting help is accepting help when it is offered. The reasons we use to avoid asking for assistance are the same excuses we use to not accept it from others. So stop it! Ask for help and take it when it is offered to you. You're worth it.

#53
Say No

It might be okay to say no, but sometimes it is really hard to actually utter that little two-letter word. You want to be a team player and you want to make others happy, which is admirable, but if you don't say no when you need to you will be unhappy and stressed out. Your happiness matters just as much as everyone else's!

Some people have no trouble saying no to others, and for that I commend you. But, for the rest of us, we have to learn to be okay with possibly disappointing others when we refuse them. We all want to be liked and, deep down, there is a fear that if you say no, the other person won't like you. If you step back though, you will realize that if that person only likes you because you give them what they want, then they are not really that great of a person anyway.

You have to remember that saying no is okay. You have the right to not do what others want you to do. You and everyone else need to learn to be okay with that for your own mental health. You don't even have to have a reason other than you just don't want to. Even if you have nothing to do other than wanting to relax and have time for yourself, you can say no and that's still okay.

#54
Limit Negative Input

Be careful what you listen to, watch, and read because if you are listening to, watching, and reading negative things, you will begin to feel negative feelings such as stress and anxiety. This became very apparent during times like the 9/11 terrorist attacks, the Desert Storm war coverage, and the Oklahoma bombing when news coverage was constant and showed the horrors of what was happening as well as the traumatic impact these events were having on everyone. People became increasingly depressed and anxious when they watched that coverage all the time.

The same concept applies to people who listen to violent, negative music; watch violent movies; and play violent, realistic video games. That doesn't mean they are going to go out and act out what they saw, but it likely will have a negative impact on them.

What you put into your mind and body, you will get out of it. A constant barrage of sad, negative, or violent things will illicit those types of emotions. So, put on a feel-good movie or some uplifting music and turn the news off, and see how much better you feel.

#55
Use Positive Affirmations

Many years ago, *Saturday Night Live* did some pretty funny skits about using positive affirmations, but they really aren't a joke. I have positive messages posted in my office and my home that remind me to relax, focus on what is important, and stay positive.

As a form of positive self-talk, affirmations help us improve our mood and decrease stress with their positive messages. They can help us to remember our value and provide encouragement when we are feeling down.

Here are some of my favorite positive affirmations:
1. I am strong.
2. I am loved and I love with all my heart.
3. I am blessed and have all that I need.
4. I am important and valuable.

5. I am in charge of my life; stress/anxiety is not in charge of me.
6. My life is wonderful and I am grateful for it.
7. I am not alone. The Divine is always with me.
8. I release fear and welcome peace.
9. I breathe in calmness and relaxation and blow out tension and stress.
10. Every day I am happier and healthier than the day before.

Feel free to write some of your own positive affirmations. Post them in your home or workplace or even your car. Put them where you are sure to see them often so you can be reminded of what is true and positive in your life. You can also recite them in the morning before you start your day to set the intention of what you want.

#56
Do Something Nice for Yourself

Take a moment to think of the last time you did something nice for yourself. Most of us don't do much for ourselves that is out of the ordinary. But, it can feel really good to be extra nice to yourself, so try it.

It does not have to be something big or extravagant. It can be something like buying flowers for your desk or home. I buy a bouquet of fresh flowers every week for my kitchen table. Sure, it makes the kitchen look nice, but it is something that also makes me happy every time I walk by and see them. It is a gift I give myself every week.

Choose something that you would like for yourself and go out and get it. It doesn't have to be something you buy. It can be something you allow yourself to do that you enjoy. Just be nice to yourself for a healthy and positive change in your life.

#57
Volunteer Somewhere

When you are feeling stressed and anxious, you may not feel like doing anything at all, let alone volunteering your time for someone else. However, volunteering your time to help others is a great way to get out of your own head and increase positive feelings.

We can get so caught up in our own misery that we forget that others are suffering, too. Volunteering your time at a food bank or animal shelter or any other organization that helps the less fortunate can help to put things in perspective. We can believe that our problems are the worst, but when faced with another's suffering, it can put into perspective that things might not be as bad as we thought.

You can also volunteer to do something nice for others. Things like shoveling your neighbor's sidewalk after a snow, spending time with the elderly who are alone or delivering meals to the homebound are great ways to volunteer and feel good about yourself. Those good feelings might just be the thing that helps you realize that you are able to handle anything, including anxiety and stress. Be someone else's hero. Be your own hero.

#58
Spend Time with Friends

You need friends and you need to spend time with your friends often. Humans are social creatures and if we do not have enough social interactions, we can become anxious and stressed.

Make sure you do not get so caught up in all the things that you feel you have to do and forget about the things you want to do like hanging out with a buddy. Schedule it in and make it a priority to spend at least some time with friends each day. It can be just texting, talking on the phone, or lunch, but have your friend time daily.

If you don't have a strong social network, take some time to develop one. See technique #94 for ideas on developing a social network and make it a priority in your life. You are an amazing person and the world needs to get to know you!

#59
Take a Mental Health Day

In times where you are feeling stressed or anxious it is healthy to recognize what you are feeling and allow yourself to take a break from it. Taking a mental health day is a great way to improve your emotions.

Once I was feeling a bit overwhelmed and decided to take the afternoon off from work. I didn't have any clients that afternoon, just a lot of administrative stuff to do. All by myself, in the middle of the day, I went to a movie. It felt really strange and almost wrong in some way that I did this, but it was a great way to disconnect from the world and my feelings and just enjoy myself for a little while. I still got my administrative work done, but I was able to do it feeling less stressed and more focused than before.

I also did this with my daughter one time. She was having a difficult time in her teenage years and we both took off at lunch and went to a special place in the mountains by the river and just talked for a long time. We had the entire afternoon all to ourselves. It really felt necessary and ended up being very helpful. When we got back, things didn't feel as overwhelming for her and she was able to face things in a clearer and easier way. It was also a nice bonding time for the two of us.

You don't have to wait until you are feeling overwhelmed to take a mental health day. Take one when you are feeling good to maintain those good feelings. I look at it as a self-care technique.

#60
Do Yoga

Yoga is amazing for both your physical and mental health. Research has proven what those who regularly do yoga have said for years: it helps you feel happier, more positive, and more relaxed, and it improves functioning overall. There is evidence that it is an effective adjunct treatment for depression, anxiety, low self-esteem, Attention Deficit Hyperactivity Disorder (ADHD), and Post-Traumatic Stress Disorder (PTSD).

There are different types of yoga depending on preference, health, mobility, and symptoms. Try a few different classes, or if you are a little shy, get a DVD or even look for free videos on the Internet. Try it two to three times per week for a month and see how you feel. I'm betting you will feel better.

#61
Visualize a Calming Place

Find a time where you will not be disturbed for a while and make yourself comfortable by lying or sitting down. Close your eyes and begin to do the deep breathing exercise found in technique #45. After a minute or two of deep breathing, imagine a place that you can feel completely safe and calm. This can be a place that exists in reality or only in your mind. This is your place so you can make it into anything you choose. Then use your imagination and explore this place by noticing everything you see, hear, feel, and smell. You can even bring the sense of taste into your visualization; for example, if you imagined you were at the beach you might taste salt on your lips.

This is a great visualization you can practice to help you learn to relax your body and mind. It can also be done when you are stressed or you want to disengage from reality for a while. It is really good for helping you turn off your thoughts at night so you can drift into sleep.

When you are focused on going to your calming place, you cannot be thinking about your stress or having negative thoughts and emotions because it is impossible to be relaxed and stressed at the same time. If you find that unwelcome thoughts intrude into your calming place visualization, simply let them float away, right out of the top of your head, and go back to exploring your safe place.

The more you practice going to your safe place, the easier it will be for you to get there when you need to relax. You can even choose a symbol of your safe place such as a word, a rock, a flower, or whatever you find there that reminds you of your place of peace and calm. It can be helpful to visualize the symbol of your safe place while taking a few deep relaxation breaths in difficult moments to help you relax and let go of stress.

#62
Get a Massage

Just the thought of an hour-long massage triggers feelings of relaxation for me, but there is a real science behind why massage helps, beyond just how good it feels. Massage is thought to help several physical conditions and issues, but it is believed that it is also good for depression, anxiety, and stress management. Beyond the obvious relaxation component, massage therapy is known to affect the internal systems of the body including the circulatory, lymphatic, and nervous systems.

There are many different types of massage including Swedish, Craniosacral, Reflexology, Myofascial Release, Shiatsu, Rolfing, Lymphatic, and Aromatherapy. Each type of massage has a specific purpose so be sure to talk with your massage therapist about what you are looking to achieve.

#63
Do Something Nice for Someone

Everyone likes it when people are nice to us. Little surprises we weren't expecting can go a long way to making us feel happier. I was once in a drive-thru in a hurry to pick up lunch and get to where I was going. When I got to the window to pay, the cashier told me that the person in front of me had bought my lunch. I was so shocked and touched by that simple gesture. I have no idea who that person was, but their act of kindness made me happy the rest of the day.

I have since paid that kindness forward and hope that the person I bought lunch for had a great day, too. In truth, I was even happier when I did that for someone else than when it was done for me.

Every person on this planet has struggles, and you never know how much your being nice to them could help. Kind words and actions are ways to show people you care about them and want them to feel good. The act and the feelings that come with the act serve to increase your own positive feelings, too. Do that on a regular basis and you cannot help but feel good.

#64
Spend Some Time in Nature

Admittedly, I am extremely lucky to live in Colorado at the base of the Rocky Mountains. I live in a beautiful town where the mountains are just a few miles to the west. With a short drive I can be right in the heart of the Rockies with beautiful and clean rivers and streams, trees, and wildlife. That is where I go when I feel stressed. There is just something about being there that makes me feel better. I can breathe deeper, and I actually feel closer to the Divine. Being in nature makes me feel grounded and peaceful.

Take some time to go to a place in nature that you feel is peaceful. Sit there and just breathe it in. Notice what you see and hear, what you feel, smell, and sometimes even taste. The forest here in Colorado has an earthy smell that you can kind of taste. It is the same type of thing at the ocean where you have a salty taste on your lips from the breeze off the water. Really try to connect with the place you are in while letting go of the stress or negative emotions you may have been feeling before you arrived there.

I have not met a person yet who says that they did not feel better when trying this technique. Taking the time to really connect with nature can be helpful in times when you are unable to get back out there. I have sat at my desk numerous times and visualized some of my favorite spots in nature. Just a few minutes of this visualization really help to lower stress when I need to.

#65
Progressive Muscle Relaxation

Progressive muscle relaxation (PMR) is exactly what it sounds like—progressively relaxing the muscles in your body. Some people like to start at the toes and some like to start at the top of the head, but regardless which end you begin with, start by tightening each set of muscles for about five seconds at a time and then relax them. You progressively move up or down the body repeating this with each successive muscle group until you reach the other end of your body.

You should do this exercise in a place where you won't be disturbed, while wearing comfortable clothes and lying in a comfortable position. The more you practice PMR, the more control you will feel when doing the exercise. Your body should feel relaxed and limp when finished.

#66
Take a Time-Out

Time-outs are typically associated with children getting in trouble, but adults can take a time-out, too. In fact, it is a very healthy thing to do when you find yourself escalating on the scale discussed in #35. Taking a time-out is an easy way to allow your body and mind time to relax so you can manage your stress and anxiety.

First, it gets you away from the situation or person who is contributing to your feelings. Giving yourself some space in a triggering situation can provide immediate relief when you are feeling overwhelmed.

Then, with some distance from your stressor, you have time to practice some of the techniques in this book such as deep breathing, visualization, taking a walk, talking to a friend, and many other tools.

Once you get away from the situation and are able to use some relaxation techniques, you give your body the time to move from sympathetic control to parasympathetic control by allowing the stress hormones time to dissipate in the body.

Children look at time-outs as punishments, but adults can look at them as a healthy tool to manage high-stress situations. They help you move back down the emotion scale to a calmer number where you can feel good.

#67
Live for Yourself

We can get a lot of pressure from others to be something we are not. We can get that same pressure from ourselves to be something we think we should be—to live in ways that we think others expect from us or how we assume we should. Living a life that is incongruent with your true self will always lead to unhappiness and stress.

The pressure that can come from others is often based on good intentions. Parents can be the worst because they love their children so much and want the best for them. The problem is that what the parents believe is best is not always right for their kids. Parents have their own life experiences and often want to protect their children from making the same mistakes they made so they unfairly put pressure on their children to change or do what they want them to do.

Pressure can also come from others who want us to live our lives for them—to spend all our time doing things they want us to do, not because it benefits us, but because it benefits them. People do not always realize that this is what they are doing, but sometimes they do realize it and just don't care.

Whether the pressure from parents or others comes from a place of love or a need to control, you cannot live your life for anyone else but yourself. Peace and happiness come from within and if you are not living life in a way that makes you happy, you cannot feel true peace. The bottom line is that you deserve to be happy and only by living for yourself will this happen.

#68
Take a 5-Minute Vacation

When you find yourself feeling overwhelmed, take a five-minute vacation. All you have to do is close your eyes and imagine your favorite vacation spot. It can be somewhere you have actually been or somewhere you have always wanted to go. Let your imagination take you there as you imagine what you see there. Notice the trees and grass and clouds and sky as well as the architecture, if there is any. Look around in your imagination as if you were truly standing there. Then imagine what you might hear, smell, or touch. Maybe there are people there, maybe you get to enjoy your vacation all by yourself—the choice is yours.

Doing this for just five minutes can help get you out of your emotional brain and get your body back into parasympathetic control, which is the relaxed response you are going for here. Be sure to also breathe slowly and deeply while on your "trip."

#69
Count Your Blessings

It is very easy to focus on what you do not have and fantasize that if you had it, your life would be better. You know how it is: "If only I were thinner/had more money/finished my degree/had a partner, etc.," then my life would be better.

What if instead you focused on what you do have? You may not be thin, but you are healthy. You may not be rich, but you can pay your bills. You may not have a girlfriend, but you have great friends. Can you imagine how much better you would feel if you acknowledged all the wonderful things you do have?

I love the idea of gratitude journaling and encourage my clients to do it often. All you do is write down three to five things each day that you are grateful for at the same time you journal about your day. You can do this any time of day, but if you do it before bed, you will go to sleep with gratitude thoughts on your mind. If you do it in the morning, you are setting your intention of having gratitude throughout your day.

The point is, if you are focusing on what you don't have, you will feel that you are lacking, which cannot possibly lead to positive thoughts. If you focus on your blessings, you cannot help but feel blessed and grateful.

#70
Use a Mantra for Deep Breathing

Pick a word or phrase that you feel represents a sense of peace and calm, safety and relaxation. Your words can be anything at all that represents those feelings to you. It may be something like "serenity" or "I am calm" or any other phrase you would like.

Once you have your word or phrase, sit or lie in a comfortable position, close your eyes, and take some slow, deep, relaxation breaths. Once you feel centered, imagine the word or phrase you have chosen as you breathe in, and then imagine that with each out breath you are blowing away all tension and stress. So if your word is "serenity," you would think the word serenity in your mind as you breathe in and then blow out all tension or stress in your body.

This tool works really well if you have done technique #61 and have a clear visualization of your calming place. You can visualize your special place while breathing in your mantra. This is a great rescue tool for times when you feel like your stress or anxiety is spinning out of control, because it works quickly to interrupt the anxiety and stimulates the relaxed response in your body.

#71
Journal

If you find that something is bothering you or you're feeling stressed or anxious, journaling can help a lot. It is a way of getting the thoughts and emotions you are holding inside of you out so you can release them. Putting them on paper (or on your computer) can help you process what you're thinking and feeling so you can make better sense of what is going on inside of you. I've had a number of clients who find that journaling makes them feel much better and less stressed because they are not holding on to their feelings. They are able to think about their issues while writing in a way that helps to make sense of what they are feeling.

Journaling doesn't have to be on problems, though. You can journal on your life and track what is going on. Someday you can look back on these journals and see how far you've come and gain a lot of insight as to how you got to be you. But my personal favorite type of journaling is called gratitude journaling, which was discussed in #69.

#72
Escape into a Good Movie
or TV Show

Sometimes it is really helpful just to disengage from reality and engross yourself in a good movie or television show. When stress and anxiety are feeling overwhelming and you find it difficult to use the tools in this book, give yourself a break and change your focus from working to cope with your symptoms to watching something that you don't have to work at like a funny sitcom or a goofy movie.

Escaping into a show is not the same as avoiding the situation. What it does is help you to take a break from the stress and anxiety and give yourself a chance to regroup and feel ready to come back and deal more effectively with your emotions.

#73
Plant and Care for a Garden

Gardening is an excellent way to relieve stress and cope with feelings of anxiety. Whether you plant a flower garden, a fruit and vegetable garden, or just a cute little fairy garden, you will find a lot of satisfaction from taking a blank canvas and transforming it into your special place.

Some of the benefits of gardening include being outside where you can enjoy the sunshine, the breeze on your skin, and the connection to the earth as you dig in the dirt. It is a healthy form of exercise with a tangible payoff you can get when you are able to see your hard work blossom, pick a bouquet of flowers, or eat your harvest.

During the months when you are not able to be outside gardening, you can plan your garden. You can map out where you are going to plant, the kinds of plants you're going to put in it, and research the best ways to keep your garden healthy. The possibilities are endless.

#74
Take a Warm Bath

Just the thought of soaking in a warm bath can evoke feelings of relaxation. Throwing in some bubble bath or bath salts that smell good and maybe some candles and a glass of wine or hot tea only ups the level of relaxation. Makes you want take a deep breath and say, "aaahhhh," just thinking about it, doesn't it?

Soaking in a warm tub of sweet-smelling water stimulates your senses while relaxing your body. Tired muscles can relax while you unwind from a stressful day. Taking a bath right before bed can help you feel relaxed so you can drift into sleep a lot easier, especially after a stressful day or when you have been feeling a lot of anxiety.

#75
Throw Some Tissues

For a great way to release some tension physically, grab a box of tissues and start throwing them one at a time as hard as you can—not the box, just the tissues! You can choose to wad them in a ball, but try to throw them as you pull them out. Throw them as hard as you can.

You know what happens? Not much. The tissue cannot break anything and makes only a minor mess, but trying to throw a tissue can get tiring after a few minutes. This is a great way to get out some built-up tension or some anger or just physically express whatever you are feeling in a high-stress, high-anxiety moment without causing any damage to yourself or your things.

#76
Cook Something

For many, creating a delicious dish in the kitchen can be very relaxing at the end of a difficult day. Whether you follow a recipe or get creative in the kitchen and come up with your own concoction, there is something about cooking that can take your mind off of your worries and stress.

Cooking is a relaxation technique that has a payoff at the end because you get to, hopefully, enjoy what you created. And if it doesn't taste all that great, well, maybe you are able to get a good laugh out of it anyway. I can tell you my family has some interesting memories of my unsuccessful culinary attempts that we still laugh at today.

If it works out, it is nice when you get to share your dish with friends or family or even a pet. Cooking a healthy meal can also make you feel good because you are feeding your body healthy foods that are good for your body and your mind. This technique is even more effective if you can get someone else to clean up the mess!

#77
Color in a Coloring Book

Connect with your inner child and allow yourself to relax as you color in a coloring book. It is one of those semi-mindless tasks that appeals to your creative side as you get to choose color combinations and focus on staying in the lines and applying just the right amount of pressure on the crayon so you can achieve the look you are going for.

You can let go of stress and focus on nothing else but creating a pretty picture. There is no pressure to be perfect and it can be fun to let yourself be taken back to an activity you enjoyed as a child. In times of high stress and big anxiety, sitting down and coloring for a little while can greatly reduce negative feelings while increasing feelings of peace and calm.

#78
Read a Good Book

Letting yourself get swept up by a good book can be a real stress reliever and a great distraction when anxiety is high. What constitutes a good book is highly subjective, but I recommend reading something that is positive. Books with high drama and pulse-pounding story lines are likely to keep your own pulse pounding rather than relax you. Then again, you might find that is exactly what helps you to escape in a good way.

Reading books that teach you how to overcome difficulties such as anxiety or stress or whatever else you might be facing can be a very healthy choice, too. Biographies that highlight how others have overcome their own hard times can both inspire you and give you some ideas you might not have thought of before. Even a book like this one can be a good thing to keep close by for times when your stress or anxiety is high and it is difficult to remember which tools to use.

Even if you don't enjoy reading all that much, you can lose yourself in a book with a lot of photos that you find pleasing, a comic book, or a book about something you are really interested in. You can decide what works for you and have a lot of fun exploring your options.

#79
Listen to Music

Listening to music causes an emotional change within us. That upbeat music can cause us to feel happy or to root for the hero on the movie screen. Hearing a song we remember from high school can cause us to go right back to having those same feelings we felt when we were sixteen. A slow, sad melody can make us cry and a relaxation tape with ocean sounds and a soft beat can relax us.

Music has been used for centuries to help us celebrate, elicit courage going to war, relax, and entertain us.

Retailers have found a way to even use music to encourage us to buy things while shopping in their stores.

Find some music that speaks to you emotionally. It doesn't have to be classical music for you to relax, but it does need to have a positive message, a soothing melody, or a pleasant beat. When you find you are having negative thoughts and emotions, try putting on your favorite tunes and notice how much music changes your mood for the better.

#80
Dance

Dancing is a great way to enhance your mood. Not only is it great exercise, which is good for your body and increases feel-good chemicals in your brain, it also can help to decrease anxiety and stress.

And the best news? You don't have to be good at it! Just go out to a club with some friends and boogie, or stay in your room all by yourself and put on some good music and dance to your heart's content. Have fun with it, let go, and let the music tell you how to move.

#81
Pet Your Dog (or Cat)

Dogs and cats can be very affectionate and loving. They are happy to see us and like to cuddle up when on the couch watching a movie or in bed at night. They are our companions who love us no matter what, regardless if we think we deserve it. I saw a post somewhere that said something like, "Let me be as good as my dog thinks I am." I love that saying because it is so true.

You might not know that when you play with your dog or cat, your heart rate and blood pressure can decrease to healthier levels. Your levels of stress, anxiety, and depression are lowered. Physiologically, cortisol levels decrease and serotonin production increases. Some studies show that people who have pets also tend to live longer and are less isolated. Who knew that something as simple as watching fish swim in a tank or stroking your cat could actually improve your mental health?

#82
Laugh

I don't know who said it first, but we have all heard the saying "laughter is the best medicine." Guess what? It is not just a saying. Laughter helps to relieve stress; stimulates the heart, lungs, and circulatory system; enhances the intake of oxygen; and stimulates the immune system. And those are just a few of the powerful physical and emotional effects that science has shown laughter can bring about.

Many respectable institutions including the Cancer Treatment Centers of America are instituting laughter therapy programs as an adjunct treatment option because it works. Think about this. If you're laughing, something is funny. If something is funny, you are happy for at least a few moments. When you're happy, you're not thinking about anxiety, depression, or stress. And the studies show that even laughing for a few minutes can have positive effects for hours. Laughing is also contagious so be sure to do it with a friend or loved one.

Go ahead and give yourself a night out at a comedy club or stay in and watch a funny movie with a friend. You can read funny cartoons or watch one of the multitude of silly videos on YouTube. You can talk with someone you love and remember funny situations or events you have both experienced. At the worst, it takes your mind off of your problems for a little while, but I'm betting that you'll feel a lot better.

#83
Delegate

Ever find yourself overwhelmed with all you have to do? Most of us do from time to time. When you feel overwhelmed with things you need to accomplish, do you find that it is hard to ask for help, too? I've heard people say things like, "I don't want to bother anyone," or "My friends are too busy to help," or "I am the only one who can do this," and several other seemingly legitimate excuses why people cannot ask for help or delegate even small tasks to others.

It is important to respect yourself and your limits. It is also important that you allow others to help you. Your spouse or children can help out around the house. Sure the kids may not load the dishwasher exactly like you would, but that's okay. And yes, your husband may not help your children pick out clothes that match and fix your daughter's hair as well as you, but that is also okay. Your wife may not mow the grass in straight lines like you want, but at least the grass is cut, right?

At work, too, it is okay to ask for help or delegate tasks to your team and not try to do it all yourself. It is not a sign of weakness to ask for help, nor is it a sign that you cannot handle responsibility. In fact, the ability to delegate is a sign of a leader who trusts those around them to fulfill their requests. Starting with something small can help you ease into it, but start now. You can use the extra few minutes to breathe or try another one of the techniques in this book.

Lifestyle Changes to Manage Anxiety & Stress

#84
Eat a Healthy Diet

Eating a diet full of fruits, vegetables, lean meats, appropriate carbohydrates, and healthy fats that is also low in junk foods can give your body the necessary nutrients to keep your system running smoothly. Food is the body's fuel and if you eat unhealthy foods, you cannot expect that your body or your mind will function in a healthy way.

Many foods are high in nutrients that are believed to impact mental health, and those nutrients are not generally found in processed, high-fat foods. Talk with your doctor or a nutritionist to find out what is recommended for you as not every person is exactly alike, but a diet high in raw or low-processed foods (home cooked) is typically recommended. Where I live, some of our grocery stores have nutritionists on staff who can sit down with you and tell you which foods are best and even which vitamins you should be taking for your body and symptoms.

I know that foods that are high in carbohydrates and loaded with fat are what many call "comfort foods," but the comfort found in those foods is generally short-lived and causes you more problems in the long run. Most doctors will tell you that it is okay to indulge occasionally, but not regularly. So put down the candy bar and pick up an apple for your physical and mental health.

Taking vitamins can also be good for mental health. There are vitamins that are recommended for stress such as some B vitamins and vitamin C as well as mineral and herbal remedies that are thought to decrease anxiety and manage stress. I highly recommend you talk to your doctor before adding any vitamin, mineral, or herb to your diet. Just because something is natural, doesn't mean it is good for you. Certain vitamins, minerals, and herbs can interact with prescription medication or medical conditions so be sure to talk to your health professional first.

#85
Exercise

Just like we are told to eat a healthy diet, we are also told to get exercise if we want good mental health. But why? Did you ever stop to think about why they are always saying that? There are several studies that show moderate exercise at least three times per week for a minimum of thirty minutes can help to reduce stress, improve mood, improve sleep, increase self-esteem, increase mental alertness, modulate the appetite, and increase interest in sex. All of these benefits can improve the symptoms of anxiety and stress.

When you exercise, you increase circulation in the body and the brain including the limbic system, which is the emotion regulation part of the brain. Exercise also releases feel-good chemicals in the brain including endorphins, which are natural stress- and pain-relief hormones.

Some studies show that the thirty minutes of exercise do not have to be continuous. This means that you can do three short ten-minute exercise sessions in a day to get the effects you want. Now you can't make the excuse that you don't have thirty free minutes. You only have to have ten minutes three times, and almost everyone can find that.

#86
Get Enough Sleep

This is an area that many feel they have no control over. Anxiety and stress can prevent you from getting to sleep as well as impact the quality of your rest. Nighttime is when we finally lie down after getting as much done as we can, and then our minds click on because we actually have time to think about things. We start thinking about what we have to do the next day, stressors we have going on, frustration at what we didn't finish, and many other things that do not allow us to relax into sleep.

The amount of sleep a person needs depends on several factors including age and that person's own physical makeup, but on average, an adult needs seven to nine hours of sleep each day and teens need a little more. Numerous physical and mental health problems can arise from not getting enough sleep and those problems increase as lack of sleep becomes chronic.

It is important to make getting enough sleep a priority just like getting enough food, going to work or school, and spending time with loved ones. It needs to be a planned part of your daily activities that you stick to because it is an important part of self-care.

If you find it is hard for you to get enough sleep, adopt a routine at night that includes wind-down time, no food or alcohol before bedtime, and maybe a cup of tea or a warm shower or bath. Guided imagery and visualizing your calming place (technique #61) are also great ways to help you relax your body and mind into sleep.

Some people have a sleep disorder, such as sleep apnea, that prevents them from getting good sleep and that can actually be very serious if left untreated. If you are doing all you can to get enough sleep but still feel tired or are having trouble getting to sleep and staying asleep, talk to your doctor. You may be recommended for a sleep study or prescribed sleep aids. You may want to ask your provider about natural sleep remedies before trying medication, if possible. Even natural sleep remedies can have side effects so tell your provider about any medications you are taking or any medical conditions you know you have.

#87
Get Organized

My mother will tell you that I was not a very neat child, and to be honest, I still tend to lean more toward the messy side. However, there is a big difference between being messy and being disorganized (something my mother still doesn't understand).

Disorganization often leads to stress as it is difficult to function well in a disorganized environment. Interestingly enough, your disorganized environment often mirrors the disorganization and chaos you feel inside. To take control, you must take the time to organize both the inside and outside of you.

Inside, you need to take control of your stressors and your thoughts. Focus on getting both into a manageable order so they can be dealt with in an effective way. In times of stress or high anxiety, this can be difficult, but not impossible. If you find it difficult to accomplish this on your own, working with a professional can be very helpful whether it is a psychotherapist or a stress management coach. Many of the techniques in this book can help you focus your thoughts, but it is still a good idea, if you are struggling, to work with a professional on implementing these techniques into your life.

Organizing your outside environment can feel overwhelming when it is very disorganized. But, like the famous quote, "How do you eat an elephant? One bite at a time," you can break down your organization tasks into easier to manage smaller tasks and keep at it until it is done. What this means is, don't look at your whole house and stress out. Take one room at a time, one section of a room at a time if necessary, and get it in order. The satisfaction you will feel can help to motivate you to keep going and before you know it, your whole place is organized.

Once things are back in order, finding a system to stay organized is imperative. Simple things like always putting your keys in the same place can help prevent a morning crisis when you're running late. A system of organizing bills and payment deadlines helps prevent late fees and the stress that comes with them. Cleaning up every evening before bed or right after dinner can prevent a load of dirty dishes from piling up in your sink. When you find a system that works for you, put it in place and keep up with it. Before you know it, it will be a habit and will help keep you more organized on the inside as well as the outside.

#88
Work at a Job You Like

Many of us spend a large majority of our waking hours at work and thinking about work-related issues (what we have to get done, our coworkers or boss, travel to work, and so on). If you are not happy in your job, the stress of it can affect not only your work performance but also your personal life.

Some would rather be doing a different job but feel stuck in the position they are in. Others might feel they are in a toxic environment because of the people at their job or the work itself. For some it can feel like their job is sucking the life from them so much so that they start having anxiety on Sundays because they know they have to go to work on Monday. After a while, that kind of stress can have a serious effect on your mental health.

I'm not suggesting that you go and quit your job tomorrow, but I am saying that if you are miserable in your job, it is time to look for something else. Just knowing there is an end in sight when you find a new job can help relieve a little bit of stress. No one should have to work in an unhealthy and unhappy environment.

#89
Stop Procrastinating

One common anxiety strategy is to avoid things we don't like or enjoy. That avoidance helps to curb the anxiety in the short term, but the long-term effects are that the anxiety increases. Avoidance is not a solution for feeling better, and procrastination is a form of avoidance.

To be honest, procrastinating is one of the worst for me. I put off what I don't want to do, find excuses as to why it is okay to put it off, and then get overwhelmed when I have to get it done in a much shorter time than if I had just done it when I had the time to do it. Sound familiar?

Chronic procrastination leads to several things that need to get done piling up until you feel overwhelmed and truly cannot get it all done when it needs to be done. This, obviously, leads to stress! So don't do it. Try your best to get things done when they are supposed to be done. Break big projects down into smaller, easier to manage steps and do them. You could also get really wild and do things before they are due to stay one step ahead of things.

#90
Have Good Time Management

Like organization, time management can be difficult for a lot of people. There are only so many hours in the day and for many, there are more things to do than there is time to do it. Or there are more interesting things you would rather do than what you actually need to get done. If you do not have good time management skills, the stress and anxiety can build to very unhealthy levels as chores pile up.

Poor time management comes in different forms. Sometimes it is playing too much and not leaving enough time to do what you need to do. Sometimes it is not budgeting enough time to get things done. Other times it might be taking on more than anyone could get done.

There are some things you can do to manage your time appropriately. First you can identify the goals you want to achieve and then list them in order of priorities. Prioritizing what needs to be done can help to get you organized. Creating a daily to-do list in the order you need to get things done is also helpful. To-do lists can keep you organized and focused. Marking off each item on your list as you get it done is very satisfying and motivating.

In prioritizing your to-do list, you can decide what is not necessary, what can wait, and what you can give to others to do. Delegating is a great way to manage your time. You don't have to do everything. You can ask for help and let go of thinking you are responsible for everything.

Keeping focused on what needs to be accomplished and not letting yourself become distracted by surfing the

Internet, watching television, or obsessively checking emails helps to manage your time, too.

Having a routine is another great time management skill. A routine is a habitual system of getting things done in an efficient way. Something as simple as always putting your keys in the same place, cleaning the house on Saturday mornings, and laying out your clothes the night before so you don't have to frantically look for something to wear in the morning are examples of habits that help you manage time and your stress.

#91
Adopt a Spiritual Practice

Spirituality is not synonymous with religion. I really don't want to encourage a discourse on the meaning of spirituality so I will offer only my definition of spirituality here. What I am referring to is creating a way to honor and connect with your Higher Power and create a connection of meaningfulness with others and the world around you.

You alone get to decide what spirituality means to you and how you want to develop a spiritual practice—if you want to at all. For a lot of people, their spirituality is at the center of who they are and a way to feel connected and grounded. Their spiritual practice allows them to feel they are not alone and that they have a great source of strength to tap into, whether through meditation or prayer or some other means.

If spirituality is important to you, find a way to create a spiritual practice that works for you and follow that practice on a daily or weekly basis and notice if you feel better. By respecting and honoring your spirituality, you can find a sense of peace in your mind and body.

#92
Have an End-of-the-Workday Ritual

Working in a stressful environment can interfere with your personal life if you don't have a way to leave that stress in the workplace. End-of-the-day rituals are a great way to separate yourself from your job and free up your emotional energy so you can enjoy your home and family.

I used to work in a particularly stressful environment and would worry about my clients and what I had to do the next day nearly every time I left my office. This was not fair to me or my family because I was not able to focus on them and be fully present when I was home with them. I attended a talk on secondary stress and having an end-of-the-workday ritual was a technique presented that could help so I thought I would try it. I always used hand sanitizer when I got in the car so I wouldn't bring germs home and I decided that I would use that as my end-of-the-day ritual. When I washed my hands, I visualized that I was washing away the stress of my job so I could leave clean and refreshed. It really worked for me. If I caught myself worrying at home, I just stopped and refocused on my family. I would tell myself that I had already washed away the stress so it would have to wait until tomorrow.

A coworker once told me that when she closed her office door at night, she imagined closing in all the stress and worry about her job inside her office so it couldn't follow her home. Another had the ritual that when he passed a certain landmark on the way home from work, he no longer allowed himself to think about work stuff.

There are many different ways people can use this technique, and I encourage you to find one that works for you. I have taught this technique to many people and have yet to have someone come back and tell me that it doesn't help them separate from their work stress.

#93
Learn Healthy Coping Skills

When you are feeling uncomfortable feelings or thinking difficult thoughts, it might seem easy to employ some unhealthy coping skills. Things like overeating, drinking too much, using illegal or prescription drugs, shopping, or any other type of activity that might feel good for a short time but make you feel worse later are all examples of unhealthy coping skills.

To stop doing those things that hurt you more in the long run, the first thing you have to do is become aware of what is driving you to do those things. Every behavior and feeling we have begins with a thought. Become mindful of what your thoughts are and how those thoughts make you feel. Before you grab a bag of chips, stop to think about why you are eating them. Are you truly hungry or are you having some thoughts or feelings that are causing you to eat? Once you become aware of and understand your thoughts and feelings, you can make conscious choices in your life to employ healthier coping skills to deal with them.

This book has many different types of healthy coping skills, which teach you different, healthier ways to think, behave, and manage your lifestyle. A coping skill is healthy when it helps you deal with whatever is driving those thoughts and feelings in ways that help rather than hurt you.

The next time you find yourself wanting to engage in unhealthy behaviors, grab this book and find some other ways of dealing with your emotions. Or, come up with some of your own ideas that can help you. Have a list ready so you can go to it when you need it.

#94
Have a Good Support System and Use It

What defines a support system is that it provides you with something you need such as emotional support, financial assistance, encouragement, or social interaction. A support system can be made up of family, friends, religious institutions, community groups, your faith, school mates, clubs, a psychotherapist, and even pets.

Oftentimes we feel that we cannot tap into our support system for fear of bothering someone, feeling embarrassed, or feeling like a failure if we ask for support. We try to tough things out on our own when help and support are right in front of us. You would never advise a friend to ignore their support system and face their struggles alone, so why do you tell yourself that? You are as important as everyone else, and you should be nice to yourself.

For those who do not have a good support system, go out and cultivate one. I realize this can be an intimidating thought, but you can do it. Start with clubs or organizations that you are interested in, as you will find people who are like-minded in those types of places, and cultivate friendships among them. If you are a person of faith or spirituality, get involved in a church or spiritual group with similar beliefs so that your faith and spirituality can be strengthened and supported.

In Colorado, we have a strong presence on the website MeetUp.com where one can find many different groups of people with similar interests and can usually join a group for free. The MeetUp website is national so you can see if there is something near you that would interest you. You can also find several different online support groups to meet people who are going through similar struggles as you. SupportGroups.com is a great online support group that is also free. It can feel very empowering to know that you are not alone, and enlightening to see how others handle their own issues.

You do not have to face anything alone. Help is available if you will only reach out and accept it. If you reach out somewhere or to someone and it doesn't work out, try again. Your support system is out there and you only have to love yourself enough to find it and not give up in the process.

#95
Evaluate Where You Spend Your Time

The point of this technique is to really look at what is important to you—your values. Take a few minutes to list your top five values. Things like family, health, charity, beauty, spirituality, creativity, education, wealth, friendships, self-care, and so on are examples of values. After you have listed what values are most important to you, take a look at your life and assess whether you are spending enough time on those things. If you find that you are spending too much time on what you feel you have to do such as focusing all of your time on work or unhealthy relationships rather than on what is important to you, it is time for a change.

Your values are things that I believe feed your soul. Your values are at the core of who you are, and if you are not taking the time to nourish your values, you are hurting yourself.

Parents are some of the worst culprits of not focusing on their values because we spend so much time on our family's needs that we forget ourselves. It's like you are the pitcher that fills everyone else's cup, but your pitcher will eventually run dry if you don't take the time to do the activities that keep it full. Spending time doing activities that feed your soul helps to keep that pitcher full. You will be a much better, less stressed person when your pitcher is full.

#96
Balance Your Wheel of Life

Take a look at the image above. It represents eight domains of your life. On a separate sheet of paper, list the people and activities in your life under each category. For example, under relationships you would list your romantic partner, your friends, coworkers, etc. Under health you would list what you are doing for your health such as exercise and eating right. In doing this exercise, many people will find that their wheel is not balanced. They are not paying enough attention to an important category, which can cause stress.

For instance, if you complete your wheel and find that you are putting a lot of energy into work and neglecting your relationships and fun, this can contribute to your current stress. But, if you begin engaging in activities that help you strengthen your relationships and have more fun, you will feel that you are better able to handle what stress is left.

There are going to be times when you have to pay more attention to certain areas of life due to the circumstances going on at the time. It is unreasonable to expect that your wheel will always be balanced perfectly. In fact, I don't see that as being a possibility for anyone, but you should be aware of all areas and take action when you notice a significant imbalance. Make whatever adjustments you need to feel better and know that balancing your wheel should be a regular activity.

#97
Take It Easy on the Caffeine

Caffeine is a central nervous system stimulant that, because of the way it affects the brain, can make us feel more awake and give us a boost of energy. It also increases blood pressure and can make our hearts beat faster and harder when we have had too much. These are physiological reactions that can mimic anxiety. For those who suffer with anxiety, they can mistake these reactions for an anxiety attack, which can trigger a real anxiety attack.

When caffeine is consumed later in the day, it can keep some people awake. When we miss sleep we can feel tired and less able to deal with any stress we feel during the day. How late in the day you should drink caffeine is different for everyone, but most feel it should be avoided after dinner at the very least. Some feel they cannot consume anything that contains caffeine after lunch or it affects their sleep. Others can be very sensitive to caffeine and even a small amount can bother them for hours.

This doesn't mean that you cannot drink caffeine at all. There is some research that shows a little caffeine is actually good for you, but just take it easy. Caffeine can be found in a number of drinks like coffee, tea, soda, and energy drinks, but it is also found in both dark and milk chocolate.

If you need to decrease your caffeine intake, do so slowly as withdrawal from caffeine can cause headaches and irritability. Some people can feel nauseous and like they are slower mentally while they are reducing their consumption of caffeine.

#98
Take a Break during the Workday

How many times have you found yourself working through your lunch without taking a break or just eating at your desk as you continue to work? When you don't take breaks, your nervous system can feel overwhelmed and overloaded, leading to stress and anxiety.

If you cannot take a full lunch, give yourself at least a few minutes to take some deep breaths, walk around, and disconnect a little several times per day. Even a five-minute breath meditation or visualization can help to relieve stress. Not only will you feel better, but you will also find that you are more productive and effective at work.

#99
Get Professional Help

Despite huge progress in the field, mental illness still, unfortunately, carries a stigma. The ignorance regarding mental illness makes me very sad as it prevents so many people from seeking help. We could eliminate so much suffering if people would seek professional help and stop looking at their thoughts and feelings as something they should be able to handle on their own, like it is a character flaw to have anxiety or stress!

I realize it can be difficult to find someone you can trust to open up to and talk about your deepest thoughts and feelings, but I also know how healing it can be to do so. When looking for a therapist, you have the right to interview possible candidates to see who fits with your needs and personality the best. You can ask about how the therapist works with issues like anxiety and stress, what their experience is, and where they trained. Therapy is about you, and you need to feel comfortable with whomever you work with.

What people look for in a therapist can be different. Some find it helpful to have someone to whom they can pour out their feelings while the therapist just listens. Others are looking not just to talk about their feelings, but to also learn tools and techniques to deal with those feelings. They want a therapist who talks back to them and really helps them process what is going on with them. Some are looking for something in between. Think about what you need and then look for a therapist who is the best fit for you.

You don't have to commit to going to weekly therapy for years, lie on a couch, blame everything on your mother, or anything else you may have seen on television or in the movies. Therapy is usually sitting in chairs or on a couch and talking in a quiet, comfortable room. I suppose if you want any of those gimmicky therapy tricks, you could ask. Your therapist would probably get a good laugh and it could be an interesting ice breaker.

The bottom line is that you deserve to be happy. Stress and anxiety are very manageable with the right tools, but if you are having difficulty with your stress and anxiety, don't suffer alone. There are many therapists who would love to help you. Don't let fear or shame hold you back from finding your happiness.

References

"Albert Einstein Quotes." Goodreads, Inc. Web. December 2014.

Barlow, D. H. *Anxiety and Its Disorders: The Nature and Treatment of Anxiety and Panic*. 2nd ed. New York: Guilford Press, 2002.

Barlow, David H., Alan S. Cohen, Maria T. Waddell, Bonnie B. Vermilyea, Janet S. Klosko, Edward B. Blanchard, and Peter A. Nardo. "Panic and Generalized Anxiety Disorders: Nature and Treatment." *Behavior Therapy* 15.5 (1984): 431–449.

Carney, Robert M., Kenneth E. Freedland, and Phyllis K. Stein. "Anxiety, Depression, and Heart Rate Variability." *Psychosomatic Medicine* 62.1 (2000): 84–87.

Craske, Michelle G., Scott L. Rauch, Robert Ursano, Jason Prenoveau, Daniel S. Pine, and Richard E. Zinbarg. "What Is an Anxiety Disorder?" *Depression and Anxiety* 26 (2009): 1066–1085.

Daitch, Carolyn. *Affect Regulation Toolbox: Practical and Effective Hypnotic Interventions for the Over-Reactive Client*. New York: W. W. Norton and Co., 2007.

"Destination Quotes." Brainyquote, Explore, Inc. Web. September 2014.

Dispenza, Joe. *You Are the Placebo: Making Your Mind Matter*. Carlsbad, CA: Hay House, 2014.

"Glossary: Therapy and Techniques." National Certification Board for Therapeutic Massage & Bodywork. Web. October 2014.

Goldin, Philippe R., and James J. Gross. "Effects of Mindfulness-Based Stress Reduction (MSRB) on Emotion Regulation in Social Anxiety Disorder." *Emotion* 10.1 (February 2010): 83–91.

Kiecolt-Glaser, Janice K., et al. "Stress, Inflammation, and Yoga Practice." *Psychosomatic Medicine* 72.2 (2010): 113–121.

Krumhansl, Carol L. "Music: A Link between Cognition and Emotion." *Current Directions in Psychological Science* 11.2 (2002): 45–50.

LaClaire, Amy. *The Influence of Journaling on the Reduction of Physical Symptoms, Health Problems, and Anxiety in Women*. ProQuest, 2008.

"Laughter Therapy." Cancer Treatment Centers of America. Web. September 2014.

Leyse-Wallace, Ruth. *Nutrition and Mental Health*. CRC Press, 2013.

Misra, Ranjita, and Michelle McKean. "College Students' Academic Stress and Its Relation to Their Anxiety, Time Management, and Leisure Satisfaction." *American Journal of Health Studies* 16.1 (2000): 41–51.

Ross, Alyson, and Sue Thomas. "The Health Benefits of Yoga and Exercise: A Review of Comparison Studies."

Journal of Alternative and Complementary Medicine 16.1 (2010): 3–12.

Serpell, James A. "Evidence for Long-Term Effects of Pet Ownership on Human Health." *Waltham Symposium* 20 (1990).

Spiegel, Herbert, and David Spiegel. *Trance and Treatment: The Clinical Uses of Hypnosis*. 2nd ed. Washington, DC: American Psychiatric Publishing, Inc., 2004.

Vasterman, Peter, C. Joris Yzermans, and Anja J. E. Dirkzwager. "The Role of the Media and Media Hypes in the Aftermath of Disasters." *Epidemiologic Reviews* 27.1 (2005): 107–114.

Vyas, Ajai, et al. "Chronic Stress Induces Contrasting Patterns of Dendritic Remodeling in Hippocampal and Amygdaloid Neurons." *Journal of Neuroscience* 22.15 (2002): 6810–6818.

Whitehurst, Tess. *The Good Energy Book: Creating Harmony and Balance for Yourself and Your Home*. Woodbury, MN: Llewellyn Publications, 2012.

About the Author

Wendy lives in Fort Collins, Colorado, with her husband, her youngest daughter, and her three dogs. She has a private practice specializing in anxiety, stress, and depression.

This book was originally intended to be a resource for Wendy's clients, as she often recommended her clients keep a list of these techniques for quick reference when they were feeling overwhelmed. When she was finished writing, Wendy decided to publish the book so that it might help others who were struggling, whom she might never meet otherwise. Wendy knows the tools in this book can help—she has seen them work countless times in the real world. She sincerely hopes this book is a useful resource to anyone who needs it.

Visit her website: WendyBeckerLCSW.com

Email her at wendy@wendybeckerlcsw.com and let her know which tools work best for you. She would love to hear from you!

Made in the USA
Charleston, SC
10 September 2016